THE GIFT
OF SHAME

Scott

enjoy

Keith

THE GIFT
OF SHAME

✦

Why We Need Shame
and How To Use it To Love and Grow

Keith Witt, Ph.D.

Santa Barbara Graduate Institute Publishing
iUniverse, Inc.
New York Lincoln Shanghai

THE GIFT OF SHAME
Why We Need Shame and How To Use it To Love and Grow

iUniverse books may be ordered through booksellers or by contacting:

iUniverse
2021 Pine Lake Road, Suite 100
Lincoln, NE 68512
www.iuniverse.com
1-800-Authors (1-800-288-4677)

ISBN: 978-0-595-44731-2 (pbk)
ISBN: 978-0-595-89052-1 (ebk)

Printed in the United States of America

From *Pappapieogene**

Earth below, sky above
Can't say which one we're most made of
At the border of lust and love
There we be

Out of all the years and all the lives
This one right now is awfully nice
That's sound advice
From Papapieogene

*All lyrics are from songs by Keith Witt and Larry Praisman

Contents

Introduction

The afternoon sun is shining on a peaceful, Southern California suburban scene in 1950. John is fourteen months old and just starting to walk. He and his mother, Jennifer, are sitting on the front lawn when she hears the kitchen phone ring. *"It must be Kelly."* Her younger sister Kelly is two weeks past her due date. Looking at John playing happily with his blocks she thinks, *"He's happy, I'll run and get the phone,"* and dashes in to pick up. As his mother runs up the little walkway, John sees the sun glittering from a broken wine bottle lying on the other side of the street. He struggles unsteadily to his feet and starts off toward the shiny green glass. He doesn't see the three ten-year-old boys on Schwinn bicycles racing around the corner or the eight-inch concrete curb. Jennifer emerges from the front door to see John teetering unsteadily in pursuit of the broken bottle, just about to go off the curb into the path of the speeding bikes:

"John, stop right now!"

John instantly freezes at the sound of her disapproving voice, and turns toward her. Anger and fear make her face look like a stranger. His shoulders and neck suddenly lose strength, the eager excitement at the sparkly glass fades from his blushing face, and John looks down in shame. He begins to cry as Jennifer runs to him, sweeps him up, and looks into his eyes with love and relief. In ten seconds John's shame is gone as he smiles and points at the broken glass.

Shame has gotten such a bad reputation that it's a wonder it still gets to be an emotion.[1] John (like most of the characters in this book) is an amalgam of people I've known and worked with over the years, and he is going through what most of us experience at around fourteen months. What would have happened to John if Jennifer's look of disapproval hadn't stimulated his autonomic nervous system to instantly shift from happy sympathetic arousal to painful parasympathetic collapse? He would have tumbled off the curb into the street, risking injury or death from the multiple hazards just seconds away. It is no coincidence that the capacities to walk, be aware of our need for a caregiver to help us emotionally self-regulate, and experience shame all come on line at around fourteen months. Our ancestral hunter-gatherer tribes needed toddlers who could be frozen at a distance with disapproving glances; glances that could stop them on the cliff's edge, could keep them from wandering off into the forest, or could immobilize them if there was a lion in the grass. Children that could be frozen and instructed with a disapproving glance had a tremendous adaptive advantage and would be less likely to die young.

The process of parental disapproval and approval imprinting knowledge into offspring's neural circuits is true for all mammals when they are the equivalent of human toddlers. Young mammalian nervous systems are hyperaroused and primed to explore immediate environments, but can be cued to immobilizing shame by a disapproving signal from a primary caregiver.[2] Human development involves the added elements of being able to internalize and elaborate these processes through symbolic language and self-directed consciousness.

Three-year-old human brains have expanding capacities for language, memory, and a sense of the future. This is when guilt shows up, where we can feel ashamed of what we did in the past or might do in the future. We have grown to internalize both interpersonal standards of thought and behavior and the critical glance and tone, which we now habitually direct at ourselves when cued in certain ways. Like most of the shame family of emotions (other common examples are humiliation, chagrin, a sense of failure, extreme shyness, and embarrassment), guilt has often gotten a pretty bad rap, but it certainly motivates humans to be true to their inner sense of what's right and wrong.

Let's look in on John fifty-eight years later. He is now sixty, a Superior Court judge, and happily married to a public defender named Teresa. They live in Santa Barbara, California. He walks into Jo's Hardware to pick up some supplies and flirts mildly with Josephine the owner. Their repartee has so far felt like innocent play, but today something different happens:

John: "I just need some batteries for my flashlight."

Jo: (Smiling over her shoulder, she reaches for the batteries.) "You always seem fully charged to me."

John: (He watches her stretch to the top shelf.) "How do you stay so pretty when you work so hard?"

Jo: "Meet me for a drink at seven and I'll tell you."

John: (He feels his face flush, and he looks away flustered. *My God, she's really coming on to me. Now what?*) "Sorry, I uh, I'm busy tonight."

Jo: "Maybe some other time."

As John drives home he obsessively fantasizes about what Jo would look like naked. He feels intense shame and weak in his body. *"She's hot. You jerk, it would break Teresa's heart. Can't tell her about it. Wait a minute, that's stupid."* He takes several deep breaths. *"I'm ashamed. What it is? What rules did I break?* He remembers other occasions with Jo. *"I've been flirting with Jo. She liked it and now I'm hot for her. Theo called them distracting attractions. I'll talk about it with Teresa."* As he decides to process with Teresa, shame diminishes, though he still feels guilty that he created this situation. *"I have to remember that feminine people are attracted to a good guy who's interested. I was giving her signals."* He feels less guilty as he reaches for compassion, and is confident Teresa will help resolve the situation. He is now actually looking forward to the conversation.

You might think, "Sure, in your dreams a guy would process shame like this." Mostly you'd be right. But some people have learned to feel shame, listen to it, and reach for caring perspectives just like John is doing. He's already more understanding of how his trustable masculine presence can open feminine people too far if he is not sensitive enough to the interpersonal currents. After he and Teresa resolve the episode, their relationship will be a tiny bit deeper and wiser. A woman who trusts her man to say "no" to a distracting attraction and to come home to her and use it to create more love tends to feel known, claimed, and safe. This is especially true if she knows how to deal with the shame, humiliation, and anger she'll feel when she first hears the story. Throughout her life, Teresa has worked hard to be able to deal productively with such emotionally charged situations.

Since the episode in the street fifty-eight years ago with his mother and the broken glass, John struggled with shame, guilt, love, relationships, and multiple other challenges. Similarly, Teresa grew from being a codependent part of an emotionally shut-down family with an alcoholic mother to being able to successfully process alarming, embarrassing episodes like John's flirtation with Jo. Both grew to use shame as a guide to love and grow. This is the gift of shame.

1. Bradshaw (1988), Nathananson (1987), Middelton-Moz (1990), Kaufman (1980), Carnes (2002)

2. Schore (2003)

1

Shame is our Friend

From *Fallen*

In the evening I saw you were fractured
Pacing and raging, your mind on the line
So I smiled and asked you
Try just one more time

Emotion saturates everything we think and do.[1] Completely separating thought from emotion is like trying to separate one voice from a choir. You can hear the singer, feel the sound, amplify her and focus on her, but you'll never fully separate her voice from the whole experience, and so there will be countless different perspectives of her voice when other voices are sounding at different intensities or in harmony/disharmony with each other.

Consider thoughts, feelings, memories, impulses, and anticipations. We can focus on one aspect of the experience, but the others are always alive, changing and influencing us. Sometimes they are in blissful harmony, and sometimes not. Our consciousness is more or less both a summation of all our inner voices *and* is the conductor of the choir.

We have an initial approach/avoidance appraisal reaction to everything we perceive. This happens in microseconds and is rarely conscious.[2] My son walks in the door, and I am drawn to go hug him. I have a mean, angry thought about a coworker, and I am repelled by my nastiness. We react to both external events like a loved one walking into the house, and internal events like thoughts and feelings. Our first reaction is always approach/avoidance. Do we want to move toward this thing or away from it?

Darwin's[3] 1898 observations of mammalian emotions have stood the test of time. More recently, Sylvan Tompkins[4] concluded that there are basic emotions that form the ingredients of all subjective emotional experience. Tompkins saw seven primary emotions that he characterized in two word descriptions defining the range of each:

- Interest—excitement.
- Enjoyment—joy.
- Surprise—startle.
- Distress—anguish.
- Anger—rage.
- Fear—terror.
- Shame—humiliation.

He added two others, disgust and dissmell (literally turning up your nose in distress), that he called "drive auxiliaries" because he considered them modulators of experience. Like the notes on a musical scale, these nine can blend into an *infinity* of combinations that result in each human's unique moment-to-moment emotional flow. They all contribute to elaborations on our immediate yum/yuck reactions. Examples are interest and enjoyment being central features of romantic infatuation, while disgust and anger are central to contempt.

Our approach responses are usually elaborated into combinations of happiness, joy, excitement, desire, interest, erotic attraction, or sometimes surprise. Our avoidance responses are usually elaborated into combinations of fear, sadness, shame, disgust, anger, or sometimes blankness or dissociation. Yum/yuck is elaborated into interesting or boring, tasty or disgusting, attractive or repelling, frightening or soothing, ego-gratifying or shameful, relaxing or aggravating, pleasurable or painful, and so on.

We can have appraisal reactions *to emotions themselves*. Some people feel morally uncomfortable being angry, frightened, attracted, ashamed, or guilty, and can learn to avoid or deny these emotions even before they consciously feel them. Some neuroscientists believe that when we have exceeded our window of tolerance for any emotion (how much of that emotion we can handle without feeling out of control), we naturally cycle through shame, humiliation, and rage.[5]

Imagine you're camping in the mountains, sitting next to a fire on a winter night. The cold is uncomfortable and you want to avoid it, while the fire is hot and you're drawn to it. As you hold your numb hands up to the heat, your body hungers for the welcome warmth, and your eyes are magnetized by the light and movement of the flames. As you move your hands closer, the heat becomes uncomfortable, and now you're repelled and move farther away. To establish more pleasure and comfort and reduce discomfort you have many options. Build the fire up or let it burn down. Move closer or farther from the flames. Put on a coat or take off a sweater. Certainly you know your goal is to be physically comfortable, not too hot or too cold.

Shame is trickier than fire.

Shame is a necessary experience that can guide us to self-regulation or injure us, but it's tricky and evokes complicated responses. Let me ask you three questions:

- What are you most afraid of?
- Who or what are you most angry at?
- What are you the most ashamed of?

Which is the most distressing question to focus on? Whichever one it is, it is likely to be more painful at least partly because of shame emotions, even if you are *ashamed of feeling* fear or anger. Isn't there something especially repellent about the experience of shame? I think the reason for this can be seen in how shame develops.

Shame begins in children as a social emotion that requires another person to effectively soothe. As children we have three options for dealing with shame; find a caring other to attune to us with love and approval, try to avoid the experience somehow (as we'll see, this is the basis of much human suffering), or, especially with anticipatory shame in response to something we are considering, comply with a rule. Since infants and children don't always have an emotionally attuned parent like John's mother to pick them up and look into their distressed eyes with love and approval, and no one can consistently follow *all* the rules, they often avoid shame emotions with the tools they have. Small children generally can't unilaterally directly self-regulate shame so, in the absence of a loving approving caregiver, they deal with it as best they can using their magical worldviews, emergent memory capacities, and immature abilities to direct attention. A common example of avoidance is the pattern of shame cycling through humiliation into rage. The parasympathetic collapse of shame is avoided by evoking the sympathetic charge of rage which feels more powerful. Rage can be acted on. I can attack someone or something I'm angry at, which feels stronger and more pleasurable than shameful collapse, *even if the one I'm attacking is me.* Shame is *much* trickier than fire.

Avoiding shame drives psychological defenses.

Avoiding shame emotions is how many psychological defenses (like denial, projection, scapegoating, and rationalization) originally develop. Most adults find tolerating and self-reflecting on shame uncomfortable to intolerable. We all have natural strategies for avoiding shame emotions. What are yours?

- Do you consciously feel shame, guilt, embarrassment, or humiliation and push them away in suppression?

- Do you reflexively respond to shame emotions by rationalizing that whatever you thought, felt, or did was not really wrong or a violation of a personal standard?

- Do you amplify shame into rage at yourself, and then punish yourself in thought or action?

- Do you reflexively repress (or dissociate from) shame emotions so you don't know if you're feeling them?

- Do you set impossibly high standards for service, work, compassion, or morality, and then struggle to comply (or pretend to comply)?

- Do you distract yourself from shame emotions by blaming, denying, projecting, or seeking stimulation like food, drugs, sex, video-games, competition, media input, or social engagement?

In our example with John and Jo's flirtation at the hardware store, John might have suppressed his shame, called Teresa and lied about having to work late, and then met Jo for a drink at seven. This is the equivalent of being drawn to the fire, blanking out the discomfort as your hands get too close to the flames, and holding them there as they get progressively more burned. On the other hand, we can amplify shame in ways that are disproportionate to events, and then actively or passively attack ourselves. We can turn shame into anger at ourselves and indulge self-destructive impulses. With John this might involve feeling like such a louse for flirting with Jo that he hides it from Teresa, becomes depressed, and can't get into it that night when they start making love. This is the equivalent of letting the fire slightly injure your hands, and then walking off into the cold wilderness in embarrassment for making a mistake, or for fear of being further burned, or in self-punishment (as in "I screwed up with the fire, so I don't deserve to sit by it").

Emotion constantly informs and guides all mammals. The difference with humans is that we have the blessing and curse of consciousness. Consciousness includes the abilities to be self-aware, to know there is a past, present, and future for ourselves and everything else, to inhabit an astonishing number of perspectives (including *imaginary* perspectives such as daydreams and fantasies), to have responsibility (the ability to consciously respond; response + ability) for everything we experience and do, and to know we will die.

One of the problems with shame is that we don't develop the neural architecture to be able to process it with mature self-awareness until we are *at least* teenagers. Specifically, around eleven we begin to be able to hold competing concepts simultaneously and to inhabit "what if" and "as if" situations.[6] We begin to have *the capacity* to consider that shame is an unpleasant experience that indicates we have violated an internal sense of how we should be, and that we need to tolerate the discomfort, discern the violation, evaluate the behavior and the internal representation of how we should be, and adjust either the representation and/or the behavior; all while accepting ourselves as imperfect but lovable. This involves simultaneously experiencing values both as solid standards we need to abide by and as fluid systems to be refined throughout life.

Five to ten-year-old brains tend to naturally consider right and wrong according to "the rules."[7] Further, they can notice the experience of shame and learn to ask adults for support and clarification, and older children can often comprehend the idea that they can accept themselves even when they're not perfect. Children five and younger have more of a magical orientation that is even less conceptual and more impulsive. They have difficulty tolerating any discomfort such as shame emotions, much less looking for guidance and wisdom in such discomfort.[8] This means *everybody's* initial training in dealing with shame has habitual elements of trying to avoid the experience, and that certain forms of more mature processing can only be learned when we are older, wiser, and more self-aware.

Here are John and Teresa after he has described his distracting attraction and Jo's offer to have a drink. Teresa initially experienced what David Deida calls discriminative jealousy, the protective anger and threat a woman feels when another woman is creating an intimate relationship with her man.[9] In hunter-gatherer groups, her mate falling in love with another woman could limit valuable resources for a woman and her children. This is in contrast to obligate jealousy that a man might feel for his woman being sexual in any way with another man,[10] a process that in hunter-gatherer society might cause her to have another man's child:

> Teresa: (She feels her face flush with humiliation and feels a flood of rage. Shame experienced in connection with another person often turns into humiliation and then mobilizing anger. *"That bitch Jo. She knows John's married and hit on him anyway. This is the first he's said about it. What's wrong*

with him? What's wrong with me that he wants to cheat on me? How long has this been going on?") "God damn it, John. How could you? How long has this been going on?"

John: (He looks down miserably and feels weak and sick. *"I hate hurting her. I really screwed up."*) "I don't know. Every time I've gone in the store we've been friendly and kidded around, but this is the first time it felt, you know … hot." (He raises his eyes and sees the hurt and rage on her face. Thirty-five years ago, Teresa might have shut down, screamed, shouted, hit, left, or even gone out with another man when she felt this bad. She's grown enormously throughout her life, but the old feelings and impulses are still there and she's wrestling with them right now. John finds himself admiring her struggle to get hold of herself. *"It won't help for me to just collapse. I need to suggest the best way I can to guide us through this. Come on. Grow up, John. Take some responsibility. She's hurting and needs love. Love her."*) "I know you feel like I cheated on you, but I didn't. This is the first time something's happened and she's never made any moves before. I realize I must have been giving mixed signals. I love you, I'm attracted to you, and I don't go out with other women."

Teresa: (She barely hears this through her anger, but some of it registers. Her first husband, Preston, cheated on her repetitively until she finally left, and she knows she can be hugely over-sensitive in this area. *"Take a deep breath, girl; it won't help to just pound on him. He's not Preston. Dr. Brown always says to look in his eyes and trust him if I feel his integrity."* As she takes a deep breath and looks at his expression, she sees him unhappy, but connected, present, and trying to do right. She relaxes and takes his hand.) "I know honey. It's just a shock, especially because of Preston."

John: (Happy to finally be on the moral high ground, he enthusiastically takes some of his distress out on someone else.) "I'll never do to you what that asshole did. I'm talking about it to make us better."

Teresa: (Hearing his sincerity, she's soothed to a level of arousal where she can think more clearly. If we are too emotionally jacked up, we have diminished abilities to hear, think, and see.[11]) "I know you're not Preston. I don't know what I'm going to do the next time I see Jo."

You can see the minefield in this conversation. If John backs too far away from his shame he runs the risk of getting defensive as in, "What's the big deal? We didn't do anything." If he collapses too far into his shame he runs the risk of passive-aggressive counterattack to Teresa's rage as in, "You're right. I'm a worthless worm and I don't know why you're even married to me." If Teresa surrenders to her shame/humiliation/rage reaction, she risks driving her husband away with a series of repulsive attacks as in, "You #*^%!" If she backs away from these emotions she might end up shutting down as in, "I will never talk about this with you again, and I will never talk to that woman again." followed by coldness and/or emotional/erotic withdrawal. Their safe path through this minefield is compassion and depth of consciousness created by years of growth and development. Here they are a half hour later:

> John: "Tomorrow I'll go into the store, apologize for flirting these last weeks, and tell Jo we've talked."
>
> Teresa: "I'll go buy some stuff this week and mention our conversation to her. God knows I've had distracting attractions before, and you are a good-looking guy. I'll tell her she shouldn't be asking married guys out for drinks." (John feels a flash of desire as she speaks, and reaches for her.)

Shame, dangerous and uncomfortable as it can be, guided John and Teresa through their conversation the way heat guides us sitting around a campfire. It was their friend. Their ability to get back to love helped everyone, including Jo. In any community it's in nobody's interests to have resentments and lingering feuds, and it's beautiful and good to resolve issues as much as possible.

Children and shame.

How about children? How is shame their friend? We all agree that shaming children is bad. There is some irony here of, "Bad parent! You should be ashamed of shaming your children!" I think people sometimes ignore the obvious. The importance of shame for children is intimately intertwined with the fact that we are social beings.

How do mammals pass on learned information to their offspring? How do young mammals learn to regulate their nervous systems? They develop and learn these things in relationship with others of their kind.[12] In humans these relationships are initially with primary caregivers (mostly mother, and then mother and father) and later include friends, family, teachers, lovers, coworkers, and, eventually, our own children. Babies without caring parental influence can either die from lack of contact or grow to be socially crippled.[13] People at any age deprived of social contact develop psychological symptoms. Development is as much becoming progressively more embedded in wider social networks (both interior networks of our many selves, and interpersonal networks with others) as it is about becoming independent. Erik Erikson was one of the first to popularize these facts by conceptualizing human life, from birth to death, as largely a series of social transformations, each one including and transcending the ones before. Most of the developmental struggles he delineated (autonomy vs. shame and doubt, initiative vs. guilt, and industry vs. inferiority for example) involve dealing with shame emotions.[14]

A realistic developmental definition of independence is becoming progressively more conscious of, and integrated into, personally important social networks. A healthy independent human is self-sufficient in many ways, but also an active member of social networks that involve mutual service.

We grow in relationship with other people and the first and most important relationships are those of infant/toddler with mother. Many studies have confirmed that a mother's biochemistry and relating style actually guide the development of her child's nervous system starting *before birth* and extending through childhood and beyond.[15] Many developmental psychologists assert that early relationships result in us creating internalized representations of parents that we continue to elaborate and develop throughout life. One major function of these internalized representations is to inform us about whether we're meeting internal standards.[16] An independent human hasn't severed his relationships with internalized parents, but instead has integrated them into a coherent self where past, present, and future all make sense. One of the beauties of human consciousness is that we can deliberately help these internalized figures grow and develop within us throughout our entire life.

Approval and disapproval are necessary teachers.

Like emotion, parenting often involves a binary system; you're doing well (smiles, warm hugs, or encouraging sounds), or you're doing badly (frowns, stiffening body, or discouraging sounds). This approval/disapproval dynamic is internalized by children's memory systems as self-approval and self-disapproval, and is endlessly elaborated upon. The more self-aware we are, the more we can consciously guide this process and accelerate our growth interpersonally and psychoemotionally.

Humans are genetically programmed to ease smoothly into this approval/disapproval system as infants. Except for the struggles to eat, breath, be physically comfortable, and to deal with occasional lack of contact with a caregiver, the first year after birth is often a blissful period with an emphasis on the development of our sympathetic nervous system; the mobilizing arousal system (our accelerator).

Until a child can walk, life can seem to be one long exciting series of positive dis-coveries and reinforcements. "Look at you; you're crawling! Good boy." "Oh, you want to nurse? Well, here you go. Good girl." "Here's some custard; doesn't that taste good?" All these are typical of what most babies hear routinely the first year of life. They are rarely censured or required to be accountable for their actions. To most of us it feels wrong to hold a baby responsible for being irritat-ing or distressing. We don't experience them as having a choice, and *we* feel responsible for their physical and emotional care and regulation.

At around fourteen months when a child learns to walk, becomes conscious of needing Mom to regulate distressing emotions, and develops the capacity for shame, all this changes.

Consider John's multi-great grandfather (let's call him Lon) on the plains of Africa one hundred and fifty thousand years ago. Fourteen-month-old Lon is skittering around a meadow while his mother is gathering wild plants and grubs. As he plays with a little rock that looks like a tiny version of what his father uses to cut meat, his mother notices a coiled viper three feet beyond him. Excited by his rock, he stands up and waves, and she sees the snake stir. She makes an urgent sound and looks at him with disapproval. He has the same reaction John does eons later. His eyes drop, the muscles of his face and neck lose strength, he blushes, his parasympathetic nervous system slows him down, and he feels shame. His mother picks him up and makes a welcoming sound. Lon raises his head, sees her warm face, and relaxes into an embrace. She looks into his eyes with love and relief, and he feels better and smiles as his sympathetic nervous system activates him back into a pleasant sense of arousal.

We know that Lon survived to reproduce and pass on his capacity for shame to John. I like to think his mother and father loved him well, he grew into a gifted hunter and leader, and died of an infection at twenty-three (the general life expectancy of hunter gatherers) after being wounded successfully defending his mate and three children from a lion. Why would he perform such heroic self-sac-rifice? At least partly because he'd be ashamed if he experienced himself as not being consistent with his internalized sense of what a good man should be.

Any unregulated emotion is dangerous: The social significance of "toxic shame."

Emotions regulate and influence everything we think or do including our moods, our sympathetic/parasympathetic autonomic balance, our beliefs, and our social relationships. If we are relaxed, wide open, and accepting, our emotions will naturally flow with our purpose of the moment. Emotion that is defensively repressed, amplified, or forbidden cannot easily flow back into a healthy rhythm of harmony and needs firm internal guidance, or self-regulation. If we can't self-regulate emotion, we can be injured by too much or too little intensity. A person suffering from a manic state of unregulated euphoria can do irreparable damage to body, finances, and/or others.[17] A chronically angry individual is likely to have diminished immune function, amplified risk for a variety of stress related diseases, and conflicted relationships.[18] Chronic fear can cause extended debilitating alarm followed by physical collapse.[19] As mentioned earlier, Sylvan Tompkins identified seven bands of basic human emotion; interest/excitement, enjoyment/ joy, surprise/startle, distress/anguish, anger/rage, fear/terror, shame/humiliation, plus dissmell, and disgust.[20] If unregulated, *any of these* can cause physical and/or social damage.

The shame literature is generally characterized by a critical attitude towards the shame emotions. Fritz Perls called shame and guilt "the quislings of the emotions."[21] Clinicians and researchers such as John Bradshaw,[22] Patric Carnes,[23] Jane Middelton-Moz,[24] and Gershen Kaufman,[25] among many others, though always acknowledging the central importance of shame in socialization and development, seem to inevitably expand into endless examples of shame's toxic effects on physical, emotional, and social functioning and development. Since these writers tend to be clinicians, this is understandable. Anyone who practices psychotherapy (or any form of interpersonal emotional/social/spiritual healing) has experienced the shame emotions being central to much unhappiness and psychopathology. It is true that *unregulated* shame is damaging in numerous ways.[26] It is also true that since we don't have the brain development to effectively self-regulate shame until adolescence (at the earliest), we all create various combinations of instinctive defensive strategies to avoid the shame emotions. These defenses range from completely denying shame, to compulsively shaming others, to the passive-aggressive strategy of becoming lost in shame. It is these *defensive strategies* that numb, amplify, or distort the *necessary* suffering of feeling, tolerating, and effectively processing shame emotions. Thus "toxic shame" has the same significance as "toxic anger," "toxic excitement," "toxic fear," "toxic enjoyment," or "toxic any other emotion." Any unregulated emotion can become toxic physically, psychologically, developmentally, and/or socially.

Maybe Freud was avoiding shame.

Perhaps Sigmund Freud focused on anxiety rather than shame in understanding neurosis because anxiety was less painful to feel, discuss, or acknowledge. Of course, we can be anxious about many things that don't involve shame emotions. We can fear the barking dog next door or the dark closet in our room. We can be anxious about potential harms other than shame/humiliation. On the other hand, injury or mishap tend to involve feeling out of control and powerless, experiences that are associated with shame.[27] Is the anxiety that characterizes neuroses at least partly (perhaps largely) fear of shame? Did Freud, who acknowledged desire for loving praise as a major human motivator, unconsciously avoid a second, equally basic driving force, our repulsion to disapproval and shame? We tend to easily perceive, acknowledge, and assimilate loving praise. We learn to avoid feeling, acknowledging, or exploring shame emotions. Perhaps this creates systemic biases that have become so intertwined in our worldviews that they warp our understanding outside of our conscious awareness. Perhaps the reason that the anatomy of the clitoris was not accurately known *until 1998* was that embarrassment at studying female genitalia subtly influenced scientists from looking too deeply into women's sexual areas.

Shame is necessary.

We are all born with temperaments that have varying degrees of novelty seeking, harm avoidance, persistence, dependence, cooperativeness, self-directedness, self-transcendence, and emotional reactivity.[28] Our experiences interact with our nature and genetic programming to guide the development of our body, brain, and mind. Much of this development revolves around binary choices; starters and stoppers such as pleasant/unpleasant, interesting/frightening, pleasurable/painful, approval/disapproval and so on. One central mechanism of caregivers shaping and socializing developing brains and minds is through approval/disapproval expressed through eye contact, facial expression, words, tone, gesture, touch, and posture. Approval encourages a behavior and evokes sympathetic excitement, which helps consolidate learning into our nervous systems. Disapproval discourages behavior and, often in the presence of initial sympathetic excitement, evokes the painful parasympathetic slump of shame which also helps consolidate learning into our nervous systems. As we develop we internalize approvals and disapprovals into internal representations that we routinely measure ourselves against. When we evaluate ourselves as being how we are supposed to be, we tend to feel inner approval. When we evaluate ourselves as being not how we're supposed to be, we tend to feel inner disapproval, often elaborated into a painful shame emotion that we either avoid, self-regulate, or allow another's attention and approval to regulate for us.

The internalized representations that begin with approval and disapproval continue to grow, develop, and branch out throughout our lives, and they are largely responsible for the fact that in all human societies people generally are trying to behave in ways that support the social framework and are "good" according to internalized social norms. Without the distress at not meeting our personal standards (distress which often involves internal disapproval and shame emotions), we would lose a central mechanism that informs us as to whether we are living a "good" life and behaving with others the way we believe a "good" person should. Shame is our friend.

1. Siegal (1999)

2. Ibid

3. Darwin (1872)

4. Nathanson (1987)

5. Siegal (1999)

6. Wilber (2000)

7. Ibid

8. Ibid

9. Deida (2003)

10. Ibid

11. van der Kolk (2006)

12. Shore (2003)

13. Tronick (2006)

14. Wilber (2000)

15. Siegal (1999)

16. Kernberg (1975)

17. DSM1V (1994)

18. Debroski (1985), Suarez (2003), Gottman (2001)

19. Shore (2006)

20. Nathanson (1987)

21. Ibid

22. Bradshaw (1988)

23. Carnes (2001)

24. Middelton-Moz (1990)

25. Kaufman (1980)

26. Schore (2003)

27. Nathanson (1987)

28. Cloniger (2004)

2

Should-patterns: Our Brain's Autopilot

From *Love Away*

Standing in the rain she saw his hand reach out
He was a dear, dear man
Where did he find roses in the wintertime?
But she smiled and took them with a graceful shrug
What else could she do?
When friendship hurt her heart but still survived

Frankie asked, "Does this have to get back to Paul?"
He didn't know Diane that well after all

Won't throw my love away
Don't throw our love away
Won't throw our love away
Oh, no

Here is John at age two-and-a-half watching a Thursday afternoon soap opera with Jennifer. Bored with the incomprehensible melodrama (which has Jennifer riveted to the screen), John wanders into the kitchen where, just this morning, he has learned from his father the delightful ability to open the refrigerator door. Walking up to the fridge, he laboriously opens the door and notices there is a big glass bowl of jello and grapes (his favorite desert) on the second shelf. He pulls the container off the shelf and the unexpected weight upsets his balance. John teeters precariously for a moment and then falls backwards onto the linoleum floor, breaking the bowl and spilling jello and fruit everywhere. Jennifer hears the crash and comes rushing in to find the desert she has just finished making for that night's family dinner ruined, and John crying in the middle of a big, sticky, dangerous mess:

Jennifer: "John! What have you done?"

John: (Overwhelmed, he covers his face with his hands.) "No, no, nothing."

Neuroscientists sometimes refer to the human brain as an anticipation and association machine,[1] but what does this mean exactly? Jeff Hawkins is a computer scientist who helped develop the palm pilot. Fascinated by how our minds function and what constitutes intelligence, he researched and wrote *On Intelligence*. In this remarkable book, Hawkins makes a persuasive case for brains as recording, scanning, anticipating, associating, and reacting systems based on relatively simple principles.[2] He believes we constantly monitor experience and automatically create what he calls "invariant representations" of how we predict everything should be. Simultaneously, our brains are always *comparing* our experience to our invariant representations, *bringing it to our attention* when something varies from what we expect, and *priming* us for a response. My belief is that, as we gain capacities for focal attention and more complex social relating, this scanning and alerting process also increasingly directs us towards elements of our environment that resonate with our developing needs and drives. Such needs and drives include the obvious imperatives of breath, hunger, thirst, and social contact, but also involve our needs to create meaning,[3] inhabit positions on personally important social hierarchies,[4] be true to masculine and feminine aspects and essences,[5] and relate intimately with others.[6]

Hawkins maintains that as our brains scan for matches between what we expect, observe, want, and how we believe we should be, we have primed hierarchies of responses to various stimuli. These primed responses naturally flow from *most habitual* to *least habitual*. Each response hierarchy is cued by different perceptual/emotional combinations and involves perspectives and impulses generated by neural networks that are established early in life. These neural networks are reinforced and deepened each time we enter a particular state and engage in a particular behavior. Using conscious will we can gradually alter the order of these reactions by choosing less habitual responses over a period of time. For instance, driving in Europe at first requires conscious effort to keep to the left side of the road but, after a while, driving on the left becomes more reflexive. As we'll explore in detail later, what is higher or lower on these hierarchies of unconsciously primed responses, and our interior relationships with them, heavily informs how we think, act, relate, and grow.

In the above example, Jennifer felt secure with John walking into the kitchen because, for almost three years, he had been unable to open the fridge and cause problems. All the cupboards in the kitchen were child-proofed and John had been playing safely there since he could crawl. Her internal representation of John in the kitchen was that it was a secure play environment. It didn't vary from her internal representation of normal safe behavior for her son, and so didn't come to her conscious attention.

Meanwhile, John had been praised by his father that morning for being able to open the refrigerator "Just like a big boy." He had always been encouraged to eat jello and fruit but had never had to lift the big glass bowl his mother made it in. Hungry at the sight of his favorite desert, he instinctively reached for it (his most habitual reaction on an automatic hierarchy of responses when presented with jello). Shocked by the weight of the bowl, John tried to adjust but couldn't. Jennifer associated the sound of crashing and falling with danger to her child and instinctively came running in. Seeing him fallen, her bowl broken, and her nice clean kitchen messed up, she felt distress, anger, and unconsciously assumed he was breaking rules since her internal representation of messes is that they usually involve a mistake or broken rule. Her disapproval was communicated through accusatory tone, angry expression, and "John! What have you done?" eliciting a shame reaction in John. His first *instinctual* response to the shame was to try to avoid it, in this case by primitive denial. He put his hands over his eyes to block out the distressing scene and said, "No, no, nothing." Avoidance is often our first, *most habitual* response to the experience of a shame emotion.

We never lose defensive capacities. Many years ago, a middle-aged business-man walking out of a therapy session we had just finished saw his lawyer in the waiting room at the end of the hall. His initial response at the shame of being seen in (what was to him) an embarrassing situation was to step back into my office, shut the door, and put a pillow over his head.

Invariant representations in implicit and explicit memory.

This "scan and alert in service of survival and comfort" formulation fits nicely into the two major forms of memory, implicit and explicit, that neuroscientists have discovered operate in every human.

Implicit memory starts in the womb and involves our nervous system auto-matically registering inputs from all our senses and processing the information into perceptual memory, emotional memory, behavioral memory, bodily mem-ory, internal working models that reflect repetitive experiences, and *behavioral priming* for how to react to different situations. This is automatic, does not require conscious attention and, when we have an implicit memory, doesn't *feel* like memory as we commonly understand it. When we remember something solely from implicit memory there is no sense of something being remembered.[7] If a dog snarled and scared me at one year old, I might subsequently be especially scared of dogs when I see them or think about them *and have no sense that I'm remembering anything.* Sixty-year-old John might have a pleasurable reaction to the sight of jello and grapes and have no sense that he's remembering a childhood treat. Alternately, adult John might have a distressed reaction to a bowl of jello and have no sense that he is remembering a minor childhood trauma.

Explicit memory begins at around eighteen months when our brain (and especially our hippocampus) has matured enough to consciously focus on something, notice it, and remember it for a short period. If we focus on something enough to consolidate it through our dreams, we can remember it for a long time (research suggests that for a memory to become permanent, we need to dream about it[8]). I might focus on seeing a dog attack a cat when I was four years old and, when later presented with snarling dogs (or for some reason I think about snarling dogs), feel frightened and *consciously remember* the event that influenced me. Explicit memory both requires our focused (or focal) attention and *is influenced by our focal attention.* You might have such a distinctive face that I especially focus on it when I first meet you, and immediately recognize you when I see you again. If I consciously want to remember your face I can concentrate on it to enhance my explicit memory, making me more likely to consolidate my memory of you and recognize you in the future. Jennifer might serve jello and grapes years after the broken jello bowl incident, remember the crash, and have it *feel* like a memory. This memory is a result of her enhanced focal attention at the time of the event. It is also a result of a moderate amount of emotional arousal when she encoded the memory. Too little emotional arousal doesn't pull enough focal attention to remember an event, and too much emotional arousal can block us encoding a memory altogether. This is why we don't remember boring conversations (too little arousal), or what happened right after the truck hit our car (too much arousal). The "too much arousal" block to explicit memory is often a central feature in post-traumatic stress disorder (PTSD), where we can have nightmares or flashbacks of traumatic scenes (implicit memories), but no coherent explicit memory of the events.[9]

Our implicit memory processes are always creating invariant representations and primed hierarchies of responses. These representations often influence us without conscious awareness that we are remembering and the responses often feel natural and spontaneous in the moment, while actually involving implicitly learned habits of behaviors.

Our explicit memory is the conscious component of memory that requires attention and moderate emotional arousal. We can enhance or reduce the chances of remembering something by consciously directing our focal attention, and explicit memories are experienced as something being remembered. Also, using consciousness and focused attention, *we can affect the meaning of current, past, and future experiences.*

Much of therapy is helping clients use focal attention to integrate implicit and explicit memory in the past, present, and future (thinking about the future is literally "remembering" the future) to form increasingly compassionate and coherent autobiographical narratives; the stories we tell ourselves about our lives. Both implicit and explicit processes are constantly used in service of creating internal representations of how we and the world should be, and our brain is constantly scanning the environment to match these representations to what we expect and need, and priming us to react to what we experience.

Implicit and explicit memory permeates invariant representations.

According to Hawkins, our brain registers experience, internalizes representations of how things should be, scans the environment, brings our attention to what varies from our expectations, and primes us to respond. Walking into a room we have an invariant representation of "room" as having doors on the walls and carpet on the floor, and we thus rarely notice the doors and carpet consciously because they fit our expectation of what a room is like. If we enter a room and there's a door on the ceiling or a carpet on the wall, it doesn't jive with our internal representation of "room," and the discrepancies pull our focal attention, resulting in us consciously examining what doesn't fit *and evaluating it.* What's going on here? As we check out the situation we'll tend to shift our internal representation for this particular room to include these discrepancies (we create a *new* invariant representation for this particular room), and the next time we walk in we're less likely to focus on the door in the ceiling. *We've adjusted our invariant representation to fit this new situation* by engaging in the act of conscious evaluation.

Consider what a huge advantage this gives us in dealing with a changing world. We anticipate based on what we've experienced, ignore what we expect (and have identified as "safe"), and evaluate what's new (or what we have identified as "unsafe"), often changing what we expect to fit new circumstances. Thus invariant representations are only invariant until we *either consciously or uncon-*

sciously evaluate a difference (using implicit and sometimes explicit memory processes) and create a new invariant representation which we will expect in the future.

We have invariant representations for how we *should* be.

Starting with our earliest experiences of what is pleasurable or painful, familiar or strange, or what elicits approval or disapproval, we develop invariant representations of *how we should be.* Since we are programmed to crave intimacy and position on personally important social hierarchies, social approval/disapproval is viscerally important to us and we want to know *how we should be* and conform to those standards. Because of our capacities for relating to ourselves (literally different aspects of our being communicating on a number of levels), we internalize standards and bring them to bear on ourselves as we develop conscious awareness. The disapproval from mother for us hitting a kitten at fifteen months (resulting in a slump of shame) turns into internal disapproval when we hit a kitten (or think of hitting a kitten) at five years (once again resulting in shame or some variant of shame like guilt or embarrassment). We have internalized the standard of not hitting kittens (and inner disapproval as a consequence if we do hit them *or consider hitting them*) and, when our automatic self-scanning finds us violating that standard, we bring disapproval to bear on ourselves and feel a shame emotion.

This is a beautiful system of social learning. Starting *preconceptually* (we have no capacity for explicit memory and only three words of language at fourteen months) in relationship with an older, wiser caregiver, we learn safe/unsafe, appropriate/inappropriate, attitudes and behaviors through our innate desire for recognition and approval and distress at disapproval. As we develop symbolic language and a sense of past/present/future, we further elaborate and incorporate this system into our interior relationships with our many inner selves, and thus our minds and bodies are constantly engaged in a process of moral, relational, and personal growth and adaptation. This process is modulated by our own interior senses of approval/disapproval, which are profoundly affected by real or imagined approval/disapproval from others. The shame emotions are as central to this process as the glow of pride at accomplishment or praise. This creates a problem with worldviews that maintain we should eliminate shame emotions as toxic, distorted, or uncaring. Our job as humans is *not to eliminate* crucial parts of this fundamental learning system, but to continue *to refine* the process to support love and health.

Invariant representations, internal representations, expectations patterns, and should-patterns all refer to the same central process of neural functioning; scan, record, expect, and direct attention/behavior.

Since invariant representations are internal constructs of how we expect things to be, I also refer to them as expectation patterns, internal representations, and should-patterns. They all reflect the same core functions of our brain to constantly scan, record, predict, and direct our attention and impulses, but they emphasize different aspects of the process. **"Invariant representations"** emphasizes the fact that our brain expects things to be as we have experienced them before. **"Internal representations"** reflects how we organize ourselves, others, and the world through internal sensory/cognitive/behavioral constructs. **"Expectation patterns"** emphasizes how we are always anticipating experiences to be a certain way. **"Should-patterns"** captures the flavor of the innate moral evaluations we're always making of ourselves and others (as in, "You should clean up after your dog," or "I should write a thank-you note for the gift you sent me").

This last moral component is huge because how we believe ourselves and others should be is a central force driving social organization and adaptation in every human society. Also, our initial *emotional/behavioral response set* might not be congruent with our *moral response set*. Lack of congruence between impulse and/or action and the internal representation of how we believe we should be often results in a shame emotion (for instance, I shouldn't covet my neighbor's wife, but Denise next door looks hot in her bikini, and I feel ashamed).

Let's return to John's ancestor Lon when he is sixteen years old, hunting with his father on the wooded plain. At sixteen, Lon is now considered a full grown man and a respected member of the tribe. Looking out through the branches of the tree he is crouching behind, Lon notices a slight movement of the grass a hundred yards to his right. On this windless day the movement does not fit his expectation pattern of how the grass should be, and his attention is instantly drawn to it. As Lon continues to watch and evaluate, he gets a glimpse of antlers and immediately recognizes a small antelope. His new representation of that particular spot now includes an antelope, and subsequent movement of the grass in that area is both expected and normal. Further, he has a whole set of primed behaviors for dealing with an antelope nearby in the grass while he is hunting. He naturally starts with the first behavior on his hierarchy (freezing so his potential prey won't be frightened away), and then proceeds through the sequence. If Lon moves inadvertently and alerts the antelope so that it flees, he is not being consistent with how a good hunter behaves and he might become embarrassed, ashamed, and then angry. The anger acts as a sympathetic antidote to counteract the debilitating parasympathetic collapse of shame, and mobilizes him to focus more intently on being a "good" hunter. This behavioral sequence that supports Lon being a good hunter gives him (and his tribe) an evolutionary advantage that is so overwhelming that every human today shares these learning capacities.

We have internal representations of how *everybody* should be.

Personally and interpersonally we have expectation patterns for how we and others *should* look like, behave, think, feel, and interact. When others or ourselves vary from such should-patterns, it pulls our focal attention *and we react from a hierarchy of preprogrammed responses*: sometimes pleasure, sometimes distress, and sometimes avoidance. When dealing with social behavior, this evaluation often takes the form of a moral judgment of someone being good or bad. Moral judgments organize meaning and also give us the sense of maintaining social order consistent with how we experience ourselves and others on social hierarchies. "I was in a hurry to get the mail and was abrupt with the postman. *I should have been friendlier.*" "That car changed lanes without signaling. *He should have signaled.*" "The waiter was especially helpful when I told him I forgot my wallet. *What a nice waiter, I'll give him a big tip.*" Often, as in the first example with the postman, when we're not consistent with a should-pattern of how we believe we're "supposed" to be in a given situation, we feel shame. We are in a conflict between our invariant representation of what a "good" person is and our experience of ourselves not living up to that standard. The larger the discrepancy between how we experience ourselves and how our should-pattern tells us we're supposed be, the more shame we're likely to feel, the lower our *self-esteem* is likely to be,[10] and the more internal defensive pressure we'll likely have to avoid the shame emotions involved. This dynamic is at the core of much human suffering. Psychotherapy regularly involves helping people compassionately self-reflect on their shame emotions and instinctive avoidance strategies so they can access, adjust, and integrate their behaviors and should-patterns to be less critical and unreasonable, and more realistic and caring.

Babies are learning machines.

Our brains start creating invariant representations before birth and continue enthusiastically perceiving, representing, expecting, and guiding us throughout life in service of safety, comfort, intimacy, and meaning. The protesting cry of a newborn is at least partly in reaction to the fact that all this new experience is totally at odds with the oceanic peacefulness of the womb. Infants and toddlers have no conscious influence over how their expectation patterns develop because they have no conscious sense of a separate physical self until around seven months, or of a separate emotional self until around fourteen months. Our temperaments (our natural inclinations at birth) combine with our sensory inputs, our interactions with care-givers, and our developing nervous systems to automatically encode countless internal representations of how the world, others, and we should be. When the environment, ourselves, or others don't correspond to these expectations, our attention is pulled to the discrepancy and we feel varying degrees of interest, fear, pleasure, distress, attraction, repulsion, approval, or disapproval. For example, when being toilet trained, a child's parents' approval and disapproval often result in her having an internal representation that she is "good" if she goes in the potty and "bad" if she goes in her pants. When she soils her pants she doesn't correspond with her "good" should-pattern and feels shame.

The approval and disapproval we feel from others and ourselves for corresponding or not corresponding to our should-patterns of appropriate behavior are inherent human motivators to be appropriate and cooperative members of social networks. Internal anticipation, association, evaluation, and direction systems of how we should be are the reasons societies can exist. In general, people don't engage in cooperative and legal behavior for fear of violating laws and being sued or put in jail. Mostly we get along because we want to be true to should-patterns we have developed as members of families, relationships, teams, tribes, gangs, nations, or whatever cultures we value and are embedded in.

Conscious evolution.

As we develop we have increasingly more capacity for conscious influence over how we represent, anticipate, and associate, how we comply or don't comply with internal representations of how we should be, and how we evaluate ourselves. It's easy to see how optimal emotional/relational/spiritual health includes feeling the tingles of pleasure at "success" and "doing right," and pursuing those pleasures by cultivating "successful," "right," behavior. It is somewhat less obvious that optimal health also involves *feeling the shame or disapproval that accompanies discrepancies between expectation patterns of how we believe we should be and our experience, and making tiny adjustments in our thoughts and behaviors to comply with our inner standards, and/or adjustments of our inner standards to reflect more realistic and compassionate norms for thoughts, feelings, and behaviors.* One measure of healthy development is how effectively we grow in consciously directing this process. This is what neuroscientists refer to as response flexibility.[11]

This obvious adaptive disapproval mechanism is difficult for children because it generally requires mature brains to tolerate shame emotions, acknowledge responsibility for violating standards, reach through automatic shame-avoidance priming, and seek compassionate truth and caring action. Infant and toddler brains are primed to seek approval and avoid shame emotions. School age children's brains add the adaptive capacities to remember, embrace, and comply with rules. Since the core impulse of shame is to hide, being seen and approved of in our shame becomes increasingly unavailable as children become more adept at hiding. Most sixteen-month-old children are just discovering the capacity to put on a "social face" that is at odds with their inner experience.[12] The public experience of shame is itself shameful (or humiliating), and children learn to hide it from others and themselves. Strategies for avoiding or hiding shame emotions include trying to comply with all inner and outer should-patterns (impossible in any human society), denial, lying, attacking/blaming others, rationalizing transgressions, or any of the countless other *instinctive defensive strategies* infants, toddlers, and children utilize to avoid feeling and taking responsibility for shame.

These instinctive defensive strategies bias our hierarchies of primed behavioral responses to make feeling and examining shame a low probability response. When shame is cued, avoidance is often the most habitual response *because it is often the best a solitary child's brain can do*. To a human with a mature brain, *avoidance is a sub-optimal response*. We can only learn the optimal response of tolerating, self-reflecting, and compassionately altering should-patterns and behaviors as more mature, self-reflective individuals whose brains have the capacities to hold apparently opposing concepts simultaneously. This capacity begins to develop at around eleven and continues to evolve throughout life. Anatomically, the brain circuits involved in empathy and self-reflection are not fully mature until around twenty-five.[13]

Shame as discrepancies between "I should" and "I am."

Shame can be a response to perceived disapproval from others or from ourselves. When we don't experience ourselves as corresponding to our internal representations of how we believe we should be, it pulls our attention and we feel varying degrees of pleasure, distress, approval, and disapproval towards *ourselves*. A pleasurable example of this would be a tennis player who is playing far better that he normally does. The discrepancy between his internal representation of himself as a mediocre tennis player with the current delightful reality of service aces and powerful ground strokes causes him to readjust his expectation pattern of himself as a mediocre tennis player to one of an excellent tennis player. A more painful example of this would be a devoutly religious twenty-five-year-old man paging through a car magazine in the barber-shop and seeing a picture of a scantily clad young woman. The erotic image is itself attractive and stands out unexpectedly on the page, thus pulling his masculine instinct to pursue and possess an attractive woman. Our young man has conflicting primed responses to feel pleasure at the beautiful naked female form, disapproval at the magazine for featuring the picture, disgusted moral condemnation of the woman for allowing herself to be photographed in this explicit matter, and shame at his own pleasurable erotic response to the image. *If he doesn't adjust his should-patterns* of acceptable personal and cultural behavior, he is destined to have the same conflicted reactions of guilty pleasure, disapproval, and shame every time he encounters this particular kind of experience. This is probable for him because strict conformist moral systems rarely include provisions for consciously refining values (expectation patterns of how we and others "should be") throughout life. Something is either "right" or "wrong," "moral" or "immoral," by absolute standards, and that's the end of it. I believe this dynamic explains why most conformist moral systems consider the human condition as inherently shameful. Nobody can internally or externally live up to the idealistic (and unrealistic) standards of such systems, it is "wrong" to personally adjust these should-patterns to be more compassionate and realistic (the idealistic and perfectionistic standards of "The Book" trump personal experience and individual values in tradition-dominated cultures), and so all must carry a burden of shame. "We are all sinners" is a central tenant of conformist morality in most forms.[14]

We develop should-patterns in real or imagined relationship with others.

While John was growing up with Jennifer and the rest of his family in Santa Barbara, Teresa was having a far different experience being raised on a series of military bases throughout the U.S. The following exchange is between three-year-old Teresa and her mother Pam. Teresa's childhood was rocky, and this little girl is not the mature, self-possessed woman of sixty we met in the last chapter. Her father was a captain in the U.S. Navy and was often gone at sea for months. The family moved every two years from one beat-up military enclave to another until Teresa was fourteen, leaving little room for putting down roots or having enduring friendships. Teresa's two older brothers, Jim and Jeffrey, were generally supportive of their baby sister but, like many boys, were more interested in sports and stimulation than intimate relating. Mother Pam was a practicing alcoholic who could be warm, cold, or scary depending on the time of day, relative amount of stress, and how much she had to drink. Today the boys are at soccer practice with their friends, and Pam and Teresa are playing in the shallow end of the base pool. It's Saturday afternoon and Pam has already had two cocktails with lunch. Her second beer of the afternoon is on a table by her deck chair.

Pam's friend (and drinking buddy) Cecilia walks by with a scotch on the rocks in her hand, sees Pam and Teresa, and catches Pam's eye:

Cecila: "Hey Pammy, I see you started early today." (She notices Teresa.) "Look at you, baby. You're so cute in that pink suit."

Teresa: (She's been having a blast splashing around with Pam and doesn't take kindly to being interrupted.) "I'm not a baby. I'm three."

Pam: (She pushes Teresa away.) "Don't be fresh with Aunty Cecilia."

Teresa: (She loses her balance, goes under, and sticks her head up sputtering and crying.) "Mommy, Mommy!"

Pam: "That's what you get for sassing Cecilia."

Cecilia: "She looks scared, Pam." (Teresa is now frightened and humiliated trying to keep her toes on the bottom and her head above water.)

Pam: "She just wants attention. Go on, get out of the pool if you don't want to play nicely."

Teresa: (She makes it to the steps and pulls herself out of the pool, still crying. Cecilia tries to comfort her, but Teresa, cycling from shame to humiliation to rage, pushes her away.) "NO!"

Cecilia: (Now she's embarrassed at Teresa's hostile tone, and her face flushes.) "Well, excuse me."

Pam: (Her nice buzzed afternoon pool experience is now ruined. Her daughter is making her look bad in front of Cecilia, and she feels powerless. Powerlessness and a sense of failure are common cues to shame. Her invariant representations of a good mother and an admirable daughter don't include her little girl acting in this embarrassing way. When we feel witnessed by another, shame often quickly cycles into humiliation and then rage. Disinhibited and desensitized by the alcohol, Pam explodes into emotional violence.) "Then get the Hell out of my sight, you little bitch!" (Teresa runs onto the grass, mortified and inconsolable. Cecilia is a mother of two children and looks with disapproval at Pam who becomes more ashamed, blushes, looks down, feels physically weak, and vaguely realizes she's out of line. Pam walks up the steps out of the pool and toward Teresa.) "I'm sorry honey, I didn't mean it. Come on over here." (Teresa looks up cautiously and moves tentatively towards her mother. Pam sweeps her up and hugs her a little too tightly.)

Teresa: "Owey, Mommy. You're squeezing."

Pam: (She loosens her grip and rocks back and forth a little.) "It's OK. I didn't mean it."

Teresa: (Even though she relaxes and is comforted a little, Teresa is still sniffling and tense. She's instinctively learned to not fully trust her mother when she smells like alcohol but, in extremely upsetting situations like this, she needs Mommy for comfort. As she calms down she does what she has implicitly learned her mother needs in these situations in order to not keep attacking.) "I'm sorry, Mommy." (She feels her mother relax as she apologizes.)

Pam: (Looking over Teresa's head at Cecilia.) "Sorry Cecilia. Teresa has been on edge all day."

What internal representations of herself and others is Teresa revealing here? She wants to be a good girl who fits into her social networks, but apparently being a good girl means not upsetting Mommy, especially when Mommy's been drinking. One representation is that when someone else is upset it's Teresa's fault that it happened and her behavioral priming is to soothe the situation by adapting her needs to the other person. If she can't prevent upset or soothe the other, there is a discrepancy between her should-pattern of what a good girl does and her experience of herself, and she feels shame. If her shame is in connection with another, it can turn into humiliation and then rage as in Teresa's "NO!" to Cecilia. If it doesn't feel safe to express anger (it rarely feels safe to express anger toward her mother), Teresa's priming is to take blame on herself by ashamed collapse and to believe she is responsible for her mother's out of control behavior as in, "I'm sorry, Mommy." This paradoxically gives her a sense of power (stimulating some sympathetic arousal) and thus counteracts the parasympathetic powerlessness of shame.

What internal representations is Pam revealing through this exchange? One standout is her representation of herself as a self-controlled, appropriate adult, and the reflexive belief that if she regresses to being an angry child it is someone else's fault. Even at three, Teresa has learned through approval and disapproval that taking responsibility for her mother's offensive behaviors is her job. Pam also believes that if Teresa is not perfectly attuned to her, it is Teresa's problem. She considers herself a good mother and does do her best to feed, clothe, and care for her three kids. She feels dedicated to them and fiercely loves them but, when she feels shame, instinctively escalates into rage at others, even if those others are her beloved children. This is not a conscious process but rather a reflex she learned as a little girl who was blamed and shamed unfairly for her mother's rage and physical assaults on her and her sister. She defended herself from that humiliation by concluding that it was unfair when *anyone,* not just her abusive mother, was angry with her. As Pam matured, this defense was elaborated into the internal representations that it is appropriate to attack others "if they ask for it," and to drink to "take the edge off because she deserves it."

We avoid feeling and processing shame.

Nobody here is consciously examining her shame. Even though self-reflection is an optimal response, it is low or absent on everybody's hierarchies of habitual reactions to shame emotions. Three-year-old Teresa lacks the capacity for such self-reflection. The ability to have the insight that not living up to an internalized standard can result in guilt or shame can't come fully on line until around eleven; and even then it requires a self-reflective culture to support the reconditioning of internal representations and behavioral priming to avoid shame emotions. All three-year-old Teresa can do to regulate shame is follow rules, look into the eyes of an approving other, or somehow avoid the experience (four of her primed habitual strategies are to apologize, blame herself, focus on something else, or blow up). Her family does not currently have a shame examining culture because her parents never learned to consciously examine their instinctive avoidance of shame and productively feel and process the experience. Pam has learned to avoid the experience of shame by resisting noticing the feeling and by attacking/blaming others. Anger or disapproval at another is acceptable to her, and she can consciously accept those feelings and rationalize the violent impulses that arise from them. Shame on the other hand is intolerable, and even acknowledging the experience is almost impossible for her. Cecilia feels ashamed of herself for somehow participating in the ugly scene and for not being able to soothe Teresa, but she's developed the internal representation that "Military wives are all so stressed that it's understandable and acceptable to 'lose it' occasionally, and everyone knows how much they love their kids and sacrifice for them." This story soothes her and enables her to avoid awareness of the shame she feels in the situation.

Let's check in with Pam and Teresa later at dinner. Stewart, Teresa's father, is at the head of the table opposite Pam. Jim and Jeffrey are on one side and Teresa's highchair is on the corner next to her mother:

Stewart: "These green beans are good. How was your day?"

Pam: (She takes a sip of wine.) "Fine. The boys were at soccer, and Teresa and me played at the pool. We had fun, didn't we honey?"

Teresa: (At three-years-old, her brain has developed enough so that she's getting better at remembering the past and anticipating the future, but it's not until five that our brain is mature enough to be capable a coherent sense of a life story, or autobiographical narrative.[15] Since negative experiences and images tend to register more strongly than positive ones, Teresa immediately remembers the ugly scene and feels guilty. Because of her should-pattern that she is responsible for unpleasantness associated with her mother, she is ashamed of the episode. Shame about a specific event is defined as guilt by many clinicians and researchers, and most agree it is a member of the "shame family" of emotions. She hangs her head and mutters something incomprehensible.)

Pam: "Speak up, Teresa. Nobody can understand when you mumble."

Teresa: (Tearing up, she does the best she can.) "I don't know."

Pam: "Remember, we played in the pool and had fun with Auntie Cecilia?"

Teresa: (She relaxes as she gets what she's supposed to say.) "Yes. We went in the pool."

Stewart: "That's great. You'll be swimming before you know it. The boys swim like fishes, don't you guys?"

Jeffrey: "Yeah, I'm a shark." (He makes a shark face at Teresa who gives a little yelp of distress.)

Stewart: "Jeffrey! Don't scare your sister. You think it's funny to scare a little girl?" (Jeffrey's face flushes ands his head droops. Jim sniggers, and Jeff's shame goes into humiliation/rage and he punches Jim on the arm.)

Jim: "Ouch! Dad. He punched me."

Stewart: (*"Why can't we ever have a peaceful meal in this house?"* His sense of being powerless cues shame and his behavioral priming is to avoid it by going into his commander-in-chief mode. Every inch the military officer, he takes charge of the situation like an Old Testament prophet.) "Go to your room, now. I'll talk to you after dinner." (Jeffery walks off in disgrace, dreading the humiliation session to come. Teresa looks down and feels worse because, according to her internal representations, she caused this problem. Jim feels the violence in the air and gets very still. He's learned to be invisible when conflict starts. Pam picks up her glass and takes another gulp of wine.)

Once again, nobody is consciously self-reflecting or processing impulses or emotions; especially shame emotions. Teresa hasn't the capacity and Pam's invariant representations of herself leave little room to be aware when she's ashamed, or to feel responsible for it if she does. Stewart shifted quickly into commander-in-chief mode when he felt ashamed; the sense of weakness associated with shame emotions being intolerable to his should-pattern of himself as a strong warrior/leader. Jeffrey felt humiliated when attacked by his dad but, by the time he made it to his room, had already progressed into anger at Jim for laughing at him, and obsessive thoughts of how he was going to "get even." Boys grow morally from selfish, to rights for tribal members, to universal rights.[16] "Rights," means fairness for those the child includes in social networks like family, school, church, or team. Jeffrey's sense of fairness was offended by the fact that he was sent to his room and Jim wasn't. Since he blames his brother, fairness will be reestablished when Jim suffers on a level that is commensurate with Jeffrey's suffering.

The significance of everybody's inability and unwillingness to feel and process is that, to the extent they don't allow and address what is occurring in the present moment, they'll compromise their development and restrict their capacities for positive insight, growth, and adaptation. A culture that normalizes the denial and avoidance of emotional pain is a culture that is predisposed to primitive and immature solutions to emotional pain. Just as acknowledging and effectively processing these emotions accelerates healthy development, denying and avoiding them inhibits it.

Shame in service of love.

What if we had a magic wand that could suddenly transform Pam and Stewart to be several levels more mature in their ability to deal with shame emotions? What if we performed this magic right before dinner? It would take a magic wand because, even though we can have peak experiences of enhanced functioning, true development in dealing with our fundamental reactions (where optimal responses become *most habitual*) usually takes years of struggle and practice. Even if Teresa's family enthusiastically entered therapy when Teresa was three, they probably couldn't have a mature dinner discussion about alcoholic drinking or emotional violence for years. On the other hand, what might it look like if they suddenly upleveled their abilities to process shame in the service of love?

Teresa: (Mumbles when asked about the pool.)

Pam: (She feels weak with humiliation at how she attacked her beloved three-year-old daughter earlier. *"That's in the past and you can't change it. All you can do is take responsibility and do something about it now. You have a problem. Face it and heal it."*) "That's OK honey. I drank too much and yelled at you, didn't I?" (Teresa nods.) "It was wrong and embarrassing, and I've decided I'm going to get help to stop drinking."

Stewart: (He feels a sinking in his body, and is suddenly nauseous and weak. For a moment, he literally can't think. He struggles to get hold of himself. *"How could I have not noticed? She has been drinking a lot this last year, and she got so wasted at Admiral Bradley's party on Saturday. My God, it's been going on for ages."*). "I'm so sorry I haven't noticed you have a problem. You have been drinking an awful lot. I've been way too involved with my command. How can I help?"

Pam: "Just understand. It was wrong of me to yell at the baby."

Jeffrey: "Are you an alcoholic, Mom?" (Jim sniggers, and both Pam and Stewart feel swooping shame, humiliation, and rage. The word "alcoholic" is frequently taboo in alcoholic systems.[17])

Stewart: (He takes several deep breaths. *"I feel bad I let this happen, and the boys get so disrespectful when Pam and I are upset. I need to help everybody learn from this."*) "You know son, you're probably making a joke about this because it's such a big deal to all of us. Do you want to try to say something more supportive to your mom?"

Jeffrey: (He's ashamed of his snotty comment, but he's being guided to do right so he reaches for something that feels "good.") "I'm sorry, Mom. I'm glad you're going to stop. I don't like it when you drink; Jim and me get scared when you drink and get mad."

Pam: (She feels pinned under a humiliating spotlight and is struggling with intense rage at Jeffrey, but holds onto herself. *"They are all being so sweet. Jef-*

frey's trying to help.") "I know you love me and I love you. We'll all get through this and be happier."

Teresa: (She feels safe, and so she can be fully in the moment.) "Can I have another piece of chicken?" (This breaks the tension nicely, and everybody laughs with affection.)

Stewart: "You can have all the chicken you want."

If Pam and Stewart dedicated themselves to emotional growth, they could transform this group into a family that faces shame with self-reflection and the ability to change behaviors and perspectives in service of love. They could learn to tolerate their shame emotions, examine them, and adjust behaviors and should-patterns from the perspectives that it's "good" to do the best we can, love as well as we can, forgive each other's mistakes, change if we can find a better way, and help others.

We are genetically programmed to perceive, register, expect, and react in ways that resulted in enhancing our ancestors' chances to learn and survive. Invariant representations, internal representations, expectation patterns, and should-patterns are all facets of the same processes that begin before birth, last all our lives, and are central to our survival and development. The more conscious, compassionate, and caring we are, the more we can harness these huge capacities to turbo-charge growth and love.

The first example of the angry dinner reflected shame fueling alienation in a struggling family. The second example was shame harnessed for growth in a healthy family. Both are possible for all of us. As we'll explore in the next chapter, development is include and transcend, so even the magic wand family could regress into selfishness and violence if either parent allowed it. On the other hand, almost any family, if the parents dedicate themselves to self-awareness and healthy development, can grow to use shame emotions in service of love. Among shame's many gifts are the opportunities it provides for enhancing intimacy and deepening consciousness.

1. Siegal (2005)

2. Hawkins (2000)

3. Kegan (1982)

4. Leary (1995), Gilbert (1995), Baumeister (1995)

5. Deida (1995, 1997, 2004)

6. Baumeister (1995), Gilbert (2002), Siegal (1999)

7. Siegal (1999)

8. Siegal (2005)

9. Ibid

10. Leary (1995)

11. Siegal (2003)

12. Schore (2003)

13. Siegal (1999)

14. Wilber (2000)

15. Siegal (2005)

16. Gilligan (1993)

17. Witt (2006)

3

Development and the Shame Family of Emotions

From *Comfort*

All of us were children who
Once wished upon a star
Far away and long ago
In stillness after dark

And then we'd fall
And spill it all
And have to rise again
Reaching out for something good
At least something in between

Ocean and onshore fog,
Staggering memories.
I swear I'll always turn to you
And offer up release.

Yes ... it's all right
Oh ... we'll be fine
Yes ... it's all right

Human processing tends to make things both more simple and more complex. An example of more simple is, "All you need is love." As a husband, father, psychotherapist, teacher, and human being, this dictum makes sense to me and seems applicable to any situation. An example of more complex is any psychology, neurology, or psychotherapy text known to man. An overwhelming amount has been researched, studied, theorized and voluminously written about human existence, relating, development, psychopathology, healing, and transcendence, and there's always more on the way.

When it comes to balancing this more simple/more complex phenomenon, I have a number of current personal heroes including Jeff Hawkins, Ken Wilber, David Deida, and Dan Siegal. Jeff Hawkins' book *On Intelligence*[1] suggests that human brains utilize intertwined processes of invariant representation, association, anticipation, and direction in creating infinite variations on the themes of survival, adaptation, relationship and development. Ken Wilber postulates that organizing understanding from the perspectives of individual and collective interior subjective and objective, individual and collective exterior subjective and objective, developmental lines and levels, states of consciousness, and types of person is the most complete and functional picture we can have of any given individual, group, object, or process.[2] David Deida suggests that our masculine and feminine aspects combine in myriad ways to organize our sense of self, our relationships, and our deepest purposes for being alive.[3] Dan Siegal conceptualizes our brains as complex systems that develop interpersonally and naturally seek harmony while being challenged by rigidity and chaos, and in the process keep integrating to new levels of complexity.[4]

Like Ken Wilber, I think everybody is right.[5] The challenge to me is finding an organizing principle (simple) expanded through an optimal constellation of perspectives (complex) to discover something new and exciting. How shame is an inherent, necessary, and ultimately positive force that shapes and guides our lives is the organizing principle of this book. The different chapters (illustrated largely through examples of John, Teresa and their families) are the constellation of perspectives that I find most illuminating of this central premise. In this chapter we'll explore development with an emphasis on shame as a central force in creating who we are, and guiding what we do.

Let's start with the big bang and complex systems.

Most physicists agree that the universe sprang into being from some fertile void over thirteen and a half billion years ago. Starting as an object tinier than the smallest atom, our universe exploded outward and the various energies of gravity, the strong and weak force of atoms, electromagnetism, and the mysterious force that is still influencing our universe to expand, began acting on the emergent (mostly hydrogen) atoms that constituted the clouds of matter which have since turned into our current cosmos.

Complexity theory tells us that when you have a system of connected but differentiated parts (like atoms, suns, or planets which are separate physically while still connected through gravity and other forces), that is open (energy enters it in some form), and capable of chaotic behavior, three things can happen:

- It will become so rigid it stops changing. An example is a diamond, locked into a rigid form forever.

- It will become lost in chaos, like a puff of smoke blown into the breeze.

- It will *transform into a more complex system.*[6]

Greater complexity tends to result in more power, more energy efficiency, and greater apparent simplicity. Thus the I-Pod is more complex, more powerful, more energy efficient, and in many ways more simple than the first computers.

A system of connected but differentiated parts that is open, capable of chaotic behavior, and that does not get lost in rigidity or chaos, naturally transforms into progressively more complex systems. Thus the big bang led to hydrogen gas clouds, which led to galaxies of stars and planets, which led to life in the oceans of earth, which led to DNA, which led into increasingly complex life forms, which led to the development of human brains *linked together in complex social systems.*

These human societies were so adaptive and efficient that they proceeded to spread into every ecological nitch on the planet, existing in the hottest deserts and the most frigid ice-fields. When there was inter-tribal conflict, human hunter-gatherer groups could migrate to new ecosystems where non-human species could not compete with humans' superior intelligence and social organization.

The FOXP2 booster rocket to consciousness.

Svante Paabo of the Max Planck Institute for Evolutionary Anthropology in Leipzig, Germany, has determined that less than two hundred thousand years ago there was a mutation on two of the 715 pairs of the human FOXP2 gene. This mutation *greatly enhanced* humans' speech and language abilities. Humans share the FOXP2 gene with all five existent groups of hominids, but only humans have this crucial mutation. Practically overnight from an evolutionary standpoint, humans *progressed by an order of magnitude* in their abilities to *communicate in symbolic language with themselves and others.*[7] Modern humans with defective FOXP2 genes have trouble articulating words and understanding grammar. Two hundred thousand years ago most of the human genome was as it is today. Homo sapiens at that time had current human bodies, a cerebral cortex, some sense of past, present, and future, and some capacity for communication, but not the elaborate symbolic communication of today. This capacity was dropped like a bomb into the human gene pool and involved such a huge survival advantage that those without it literally died out; they simply could not compete.

*Inter*personally, when you and I engage in symbolic communication there are potentially infinite perspectives that we can share. *Intra*personally, as I communicate symbolically with myself, different parts of me can engage in a potentially infinite number of connections, or interior relationships, each capable of approval or disapproval. Think of standing between two mirrors and seeing endless repetitions of yourself; only, in this case, *each one is different in some fashion, and all of them are connected.* Your frightened self right now can consider your current sad self, who can connect with the angry self you remember from yesterday, who can consider the relaxed self you anticipate next week, who you imagine sympathetically remembering your frightened self of today. In human infants the ability to be aware of the past, present, and future combined with the capacity for symbolic language is associated with the development of *conscious awareness.* Most developmentalists agree that our elaborate intrapersonal relationships within ourselves are evoked, nurtured, and guided by interpersonal relationships with caregivers from conception onward.

I believe that consciousness exists inside these elaborate interior relationships we have with ourselves; guided and nurtured in us by relationships with caregivers. Within these infinite interior relationships the mystery of consciousness floats, relates, and constantly transforms. A paradox of consciousness is that in the midst of this constant flux and change there is some basic aspect of who we are, the *flavor* of our unique self, which feels subjectively unchanging from birth to death.

Consciousness allows us to direct our personal evolution.

With the advent of a consciousness capable of perceiving and inhabiting infinite intrapersonal and interpersonal perspectives, *for the first time since the big bang,* a complex system (a human's consciousness) could, from a self-aware perspective, deliberately direct it's own evolutionary development from birth to death on a variety of developmental lines. Further, the *complex systems of human societies* could direct their own evolution. Species that have competitive edges tend to spread farther, develop more effective weapons against other species, and become more symbiotic with their environments. Since that moment, less than two hundred thousand years ago (the blink of an eye in terms of evolutionary history), the human species has spread *off the planet* to the moon and Mars, has developed the atomic bomb, and is currently embracing an ecological consciousness where it is beautiful, good, and true to progressively more people and societies to live symbiotically within the Earth's ecosystems.

Contrary to some perspectives, primitive tribes did not necessarily have a deeper, more caring relationship with nature than modern cultures. Identification with, and responsibility for, all other people or life in general is not typical of indigenous hunter/gatherer and horticultural cultures, which tend to be extremely ethnocentric. When the aborigines arrived in Australia fifty thousand years ago, there were fifty species of large land animals that *all became extinct within a hundred years.* The aborigines apparently had no conscious responsibility for maintaining diversity of species. It would take thousands of years of evolution, aided by writing, science, art, the enlightenment, the technological revolution, and the informational revolution (via computers, the internet, and global awareness) to expand the human collective consciousness enough to feel a sense of responsibility to live symbiotically within our ecosystems.

Shame creates a reproductive advantage.

On the most basic level, shame emotions are a potent social learning and bonding system that all mammals share. The shame emotions in humans are elaborated through development to support an intricate web of internal representations of how we and others should be; thus constituting central forces in organizing and maintaining social systems. As our brains mature, we develop the capacities to use shame emotions as guides to consciously direct and accelerate our growth. This is one aspect of how we can guide our personal evolution. Let's examine how these capacities might influence the evolution of the complex systems of our social networks.

Shame both connects and differentiates in social systems

As we explored earlier, a complex system is composed of a number of differentiated but connected parts, is open in that it receives energy and input from the outside, and is capable of chaotic behavior without becoming permanently lost in rigidity or chaos. Such a system naturally periodically shifts into more stable and complex organizational patterns that include and transcend previous patterns. All mammals are social (drawn to affiliate with others of their kind), and all mammals are capable of the physiological experience of shame (separation through disapproval). The members of a family or tribe constitute connected but differentiated parts. One function of shame is that it separates, or differentiates, group members within a social context. In addition to enhancing learning and regulating behavior through first external and then internal disapproval, shame, and the fear of shame, keeps individuals separate in social systems, and enforces hierarchies. The private does not walk up to the general and slap him on the back. He would be ashamed to be so familiar with such a high status individual. Your and my capacities for disapproval keep us aware of our differences and vigilant at our potential threats from each other, while also desiring approval from each other. Varying combinations of approval and disapproval combined with shared beliefs about individual status are basic forces that maintain social hierarchies; complex open systems consisting of differentiated parts that, if they don't get locked into rigidity or dispersed into chaos, will naturally keep transforming into more complex, more energy efficient systems that include and transcend previous systems. This movement towards more complexity can be seen historically in the progression from hunter/gatherer, to horticultural, to agrarian, to technological, to informational cultures over the last ten thousand years.

Humans' needs for contact, sexuality, and social approval pull us together. Our fears of harm and shame keep us separate, and yet also motivate us to cooperate, care, and seek approval. Every social force needs a counteracting element, or it potentially accelerates out of control. Approval encourages and energizes, while disapproval discourages and de-energizes. On many developmental lines (such as the moral line of what we believe is right/wrong, and the values line of what we find important), our should-patterns are organized around how we've learned to believe we *should* be. We are conditioned by pleasure at positive recognition from others and ourselves for meeting or exceeding standards, and pain at disapproval from others and ourselves for not being consistent with internal representations of how we and others should be. In most societies, hierarchies are organized around what positions members strive to occupy by complying with external and internal standards. We comply with social rules at least partly because of shame and fear of shame at being witnessed (by self and/or others) not complying with such standards. I believe shame to be a necessary ingredient in maintaining individuals and groups as complex systems. It connects us with our desires for positive recognition, and it differentiates us as we disapprove of, or are disapproved of, by others.

Development is *include* and transcend.

There are a number of developmental lines that we all share to some extent and, born with our different temperaments, gifts, strengths, weaknesses, and social milieus, we develop on these lines throughout life. Physically we begin as a fertilized ovum that expands into fetus, infant, toddler, child, adolescent, and adult. Morally we begin selfish, and then become more caring and respectful of others' rights. Interpersonally we are born unaware of ourselves as autonomous beings and completely dependent on caregivers, and grow to increasing awareness of ourselves as autonomous beings and yet interdependent with many people. Cognitively we begin with only our implicit, reflexive emotional/behavioral/bodily memory absorbing and processing data, and develop conscious explicit memory, magical thinking, concrete black and white reasoning, and then more relativistic (shades of gray) formal operational capacities that can hold opposing concepts simultaneously and inhabit "what if" scenarios.

We never lose any capacity that we've had. The most altruistic adult has selfish moments. The most disciplined formal operational intellect has occasional periods of magical thinking. The most self-possessed and self-regulating grown-up has moments of infantile self-indulgence or collapse. Thus development is an include and transcend process whereby as we grow we subsume our current tendencies and capacities into wider frameworks that add new understanding and possibilities, but never completely leave past tendencies and capacities behind.[8]

How does this include and transcend process apply to shame?

The shame family of emotions.

Empirical research indicates that genetic programming and congenital influences in the womb combine to result in varying temperamental tendencies toward harm-avoidance, novelty seeking, dependence, persistence, cooperativeness, self-directedness, self-transcendence, and emotional reactivity.[9] In our families we develop characteristic secure or insecure attachment styles with primary care-givers. Secure attachment is when an infant gets the attention and separation she needs for optimal development, while insecure attachment involves an infant getting too little, too much, or the wrong kind of attention and separation she needs, resulting in sub-optimal development. Your genetically determined development, plus your temperamental tendencies, plus your attachment styles with primary caregivers, plus your life experiences, plus your increasing conscious participation, result in the unique personality that is you.[10]

The first year of life is usually positive and exciting for baby. In American culture this period is often very hard on parents. The hunter-gatherer societies we evolved from had multiple adults and older children sharing in child rearing, and thus modern parents (especially mothers), genetically primed to raise babies in a supportive tribal environment, are prone to exhaustion, depression, and self-doubt in response to their innate sense that something is missing. On the other hand, parents are predisposed to love babies. The shape of a baby (the big head and little body) evokes caring feelings in humans. Mothers and fathers of infants have drops in testosterone (a competition, aggression hormone) and spikes in oxytocin and vasopressin (bonding, affiliation hormones) in response to the sight, sound, and smell of babies.[11] A child's sympathetic nervous system (the excitatory part of the autonomic nervous system: the accelerator) is particularly active during a child's first year of life, and baby and parents spend a lot of time looking into each other's eyes with excitement and delight.[12]

As we illustrated with John and his ancestor Lon, this all changes at around fourteen months when baby starts walking and simultaneously experiences emotional separateness from mother and the necessity of maternal contact and approval for regulating emotions. Now the parasympathetic nervous system (the inhibitory part of the autonomic nervous system: the brakes) becomes more active. One aspect of this is the capacity for shame that allows a mother to influence (and especially slow down and stop) a toddler at a distance with a disapproving look.

Many researchers maintain that shame occurs with the intersection of sympathetic arousal (John happily running towards the broken bottle, or Lon excited about his little rock) with unexpected disapproval (their mothers' alarmed negative reactions).[13] This results in the characteristic parasympathetic collapse of shame; slack face, reduced tone in neck and shoulder muscles, lowered gaze, blush, lowered metabolism, and painful sensation. Toddlers need a caring parent to look into their eyes with love and approval to regulate this state. In the presence of such attention, a child's nervous system usually shifts from parasympathetic collapse to pleasurable sympathetic arousal *in around ten seconds.* If not regulated, shame can persist and actually damage children's nervous systems.[14] As children age, most developmentalists maintain that shame becomes elaborated into an extended family of painful emotions including guilt, humiliation, embarrassment, inadequacy, powerlessness, rejection, intimidation, extreme shyness, self-loathing, failure, and pretty much any other experience of being down on ourselves or experiencing others as down on us.

Each member of the "shame family of emotions" seems to be a variation on the theme of distress in response to disapproval, and we can enter each of them from almost any state. We have an internal representation of how we should be, we experience ourselves as not jiving with our representation, we feel disapproved of by others or ourselves, and we feel some flavor of shame. I disagree with theorists who maintain that we need to be in a positively charged state to have disapproval result in shame.[15] My personal and professional experience is that shame can arise from any state if an individual feels sufficiently dissed. Most therapists have observed depressed clients, clearly not in a positively charged state, plunge into shame or guilt when they feel criticized or attacked, or are confronted with perceived failures, mistakes, or weaknesses.

Keep it simple.

What is the purpose of all emotion? To help us survive and reproduce by giving us an ongoing commentary on the safety, dangerousness, attractiveness or repulsiveness of everything we experience (including ourselves), and in cuing hierarchies of adaptive behaviors so that we can be safe, relate, self-regulate, and grow. Emotions are necessary cues for eliciting the behavioral priming associated with implicit and explicit memories and internal representations. They help activate neural networks that tell us when and how to act, and they tell us when we have acted enough. Emotions are central to the self-regulation process.

On the other hand, with consciousness has come capacities and predispositions to suppress, obsess, deny, project, and amplify in the past/present/future. Further, we have moral standards of appropriate and inappropriate emotions; natural offshoots of internal representations about how we *should* feel, and what is *safe* to feel. Many emotions (like fear, anger, pride, sexual desire, sadness, contempt, shame, disgust, or a subjective sense of being out of control) can themselves be reacted to (because they are painful and/or unacceptable to varying degrees) by denying, lying, fleeing, projecting, collapsing, or attacking.

Shame is an innate capacity that begins as a social emotion. We feel it as infants in the presence of external disapproval, and require external approval to be regulated back to a comfortable state of arousal. If another person can't or won't provide such regulation, we can feel hammered and out of control by their disapproval, then humiliated, and then rageful. Rage can help us partially self-regulate back to sympathetic arousal by attacking something or someone, like Teresa attacked Cecilia by the pool. Our nervous systems know that we can't stay in a state of shame without risking damage to our brains and bodies, and so rage is cued to provide the sympathetic arousal we need to counteract shame's parasympathetic collapse. It's an inferior regulator because rage itself is toxic if we experience too much of it[16], but at least it is a mobilizing emotion we can act on that feels strong as opposed to the crushing immobilizing weakness of shame.

As children develop memory and a sense of self, they can feel shame or guilt for something they did in the past or might do in the future. Anticipating the future is neurologically remembering the future, using the same brain structures and processes as remembering the past (some refer to brains as "anticipation and association machines"[17]). Once again, in the absence of another to regulate us, what are we to do? If we feel shame/guilt/humiliation in the presence of another, we can co-regulate through attunement with that person, self-soothe in some fashion, or cycle through humiliation/rage until we can do something (often attack another or ourselves). If a child is alone or if caregivers *cannot* or *will not* provide approving contact, he'll instinctively try to avoid the shame experience any way he can. He'll try to forget (suppress), explain to himself how he is justified (rationalize), blame someone else (scapegoat), decide someone else is engaging in shameful behavior instead of him (project), or mobilize any one of a number of other avoidance strategies. In extreme cases, he might project his shame on another and then try to destroy that other emotionally or even physically. This is called projective identification and is characteristic of people that were shamed early and often in their development.

The optimal response to shame is self-reflection, followed by adjustment of our behavior to meet our should-patterns, and/or adjustment of our should-patterns to be more realistic and compassionate. Self-reflection plus adjustment of behavior and/or should-patterns requires cognitive abilities that don't show up developmentally until at least teen years, plus flexible moral environments that are rare. If our family, school, or social cultures have no provision for adjusting should-patterns, we will not be optimally supported in refining our values. As a result, most of us learn to avoid shameful thoughts, feelings, memories, and experiences with a variety of strategies like the ones listed above. *By adulthood we have practiced these strategies thousands of times, thus deepening the neural networks involved with them, and blocking potential shame growth experiences of self-reflection and adjustment of behavior and/or perspective.* The very emotion that evolved to guide us in being socially effective and true to ourselves is now at the core of our blocks to growth and development.

Shame at different developmental stages.

Let's check in with John, Lon, and Teresa as they deal with shame at different stages of development:

Here is Teresa at five, playing with Cecilia's five-year-old son Sam in Pam's bedroom while Cecilia and Pam are in the kitchen drinking beer and talking. Sam is proudly showing Teresa his penis, and Teresa has taken off her dress and is showing Sam her "gina." Both kids feel a little secretive because, by five, they've had lots of messages about nudity being taboo, but the excitement and intimacy of looking and touching these forbidden areas is absorbing enough that they're lost in the game. Both are in a pleasant, mildly erotic flow state. Meanwhile in the kitchen, Pam decides to show Cecilia the new perfume that Stewart bought her for her birthday and walks into the bedroom, abruptly intruding on the children's game:

Pam: (Teresa and Sam naked, looking and touching, does not meet her should-pattern of what "good" girls and boys do. Further, just the experience of unexpected nudity and intimate touching between children is profoundly disturbing, especially under the influence of three beers, and exceeds her window of tolerance for distressing emotion. She quickly cycles through shame and humiliation into rage. With no capacity for self-reflective processing, she acts impulsively and grabs Teresa, jerking her off of the floor.) "What do you think you're doing?"

Teresa: (Humiliated, she collapses into distressed incoherence and tries to make the whole experience disappear.) "I don't know."

Pam: (Completely misinterpreting what Teresa means, she angrily spanks her on her bare bottom four or five times.) "Don't lie to me. Bad girl! Cecilia, you'd better get in here."

Teresa: (Now she's terrified as well as humiliated.) "I'm sorry Mommy, I'm sorry. We were just playing."

Pam: "Just playing? Acting like a cheap slut isn't playing. And you too, Sam. Put on your damn clothes."

Cecilia: (As she walks into the scene, she feels ashamed of her naked son and somehow like a failure for this situation happening. She cycles through shame and humiliation into rage and looks for someone to attack.) "Sam, what *in the world* were you thinking? Who's idea was this?"

Sam: (He's overwhelmed, frightened at the violence of Pam spanking Teresa, and instinctively tries to avoid his humiliation with blame.) "Teresa said she wanted to show me her 'gina.'" (Cecilia looks accusingly at Teresa who is literally struck dumb. It was both children's idea to play looking/touching, but there is no way Teresa can think or talk in this overwhelmed state. She just hangs her head.)

Pam: (She's so embarrassed that she can't look Cecilia in the eyes, and her distress adds to her anger at Teresa.) "Just wait till your father comes home. I'm sorry Cecilia. You and Sam better go. Teresa, you go to your room. I'll deal with you later." (Internally she feels helpless and like a failure. *"Boy, do I need a drink."*)

What should-patterns, internal representations, are being developed and rein-forced in this scene? Displaying or touching genitals, having sexual feelings, or talking explicitly about such experiences are not consistent with the mothers' "good girl" or "good boy" internal representations. Having a child that plays looking/touching sexual games is not consistent with Pam and Cecilia's "good mother" should-patterns. Everybody was ashamed and tried to avoid the experi-ence. Later that afternoon, after dealing with Teresa's hysterical tears, and feeling increasing guilt about hitting her and calling her a "cheap slut," Pam told Teresa that "It would upset Daddy too much, so let's just keep this a secret and you never do it again, OK?" Cecilia didn't shame Sam any further, but couldn't talk to him about the embarrassing experience. He was wise enough to keep it to him-self and, even though it made him feel guilty, he continued to engage in looking/touching play with other same-age children throughout his development *and was never again caught by an adult.* This play finally transformed into more mature sexuality when, as a fourteen-year-old, he started having make-out sessions with his girlfriend. Both Pam and Cecilia avoided discussing the incident with each other or their husbands.

Teresa was *never again* naked in front of a boy until she was seventeen years old, and then it was when she and her boyfriend Preston got drunk and had oral sex in the back of his car. This episode, when she guiltily remembered it in a hung-over state the next day, further reinforced her shame at being naked and sexual. Pam could never abide Teresa in "sexy" clothes *for the rest of her life.* When, at thirty-four, Teresa showed Pam her wedding dress, Pam's first com-ment was, "Don't you think it's a little too revealing?"

In this example there was no self-reflection or adjustment of anyone's expecta-tion patterns of how children should experience, display, or experiment with their own and other kid's genitals, or of how mothers could optimally process such experiences internally, with their friends, their husbands, or their children. Everyone was stuck in primitive avoidance shame reactions, and so everyone's opportunity for growth was wasted.

What if Pam and Cecilia were more self-aware, flexible, and self-regulating in their experience of shame? This is how the episode might have gone:

Pam: (She walks in on the game and feels a rush of embarrassment. Her face flushes and she has an impulse to violently interrupt the children. Instead, she self-regulates. *"They're little kids and they're exploring their bodies. Just relax and don't freak them out."*) "Hi kids, what's up?"

Sam: (He's embarrassed, but reassured by Pam's reasonable tone. He doesn't feel major disapproval, and so he answers in a complementary, matter-of-fact tone.) "We were playing the naked game."

Teresa: (Initially distressed when Pam walked in, she's now feeling safer and chimes in.) "I was showing him my 'gina. Sam has a penis. Girls don't have penises."

Pam: "No they don't, but they do have vaginas and, when they grow up, they have breasts. Boys don't get breasts when they grow up."

Cecilia: (She walks into a calm scene, and Pam fills her in.) "Well, I'm sorry kids, but it's against the rules to play naked looking/touching games until you're a teenager and have a boyfriend or a girlfriend."

Teresa: (In this non-threatening environment, she's interested.) "Why?"

Pam: "It's the rules of this country. Some people get ashamed or mad when kids play looking/touching."

Teresa: "Are you mad, Mommy?"

Pam: "No sweetheart. I'm a little embarrassed. My mother never let me play naked games and so I'm not used to it. When I grew up and got married I had to learn how. Your daddy really helped."

Cecilia: "Do you guys want to go to the pool? It's pretty hot today."

Sam: "O boy! Can Teresa come?"

Cecilia: "Sure, if it's OK with her Mommy."

This is how shame reactions can be processed when grown-ups can self-regulate their embarrassment and support children dealing with difficult or shameful events with the intent of promoting everybody's best interests. Unfortunately for Teresa, this rarely happened in her family of origin. Fortunately for her, John, and their children, she learned how to do it as an adult.

While Teresa was growing up on one military base after another, John and his family were living in the same house in Santa Barbara, California. John had a brother, Alfred, who was two years younger and somewhat wild. Researchers have determined that there are three general kinds of babies, easy, hard, and shy. John was easy, and Alfred was hard. John's father, Michael, was a successful mathematics professor who was distant, mostly uninvolved with the boys' early childhood, but fair and kind with them. Jennifer, a pillar of the local Lutheran Congregation, had the internal representation of her family being perfect and her life being the epitome of morally sound existence. This all came crashing down just after John's fifteenth birthday when Jennifer, within the same month, discovered that Michael was having an affair with a graduate student, and that Alfred was smoking pot and drinking with his friends. The way that she found out about Alfred was particularly humiliating. While intoxicated on marijuana, he and two other boys were arrested for trying to shoplift a quart of vodka from the local supermarket. The following exchange is from their third therapy session with a family therapist, Judith, who was recommended to them by the University Counseling Center:

Judith: "How's everybody doing?"

Jennifer: (The mortification and rage of the last two months have taken a toll on her emotionally and physically. She's lost eight pounds, is too embarrassed to go to church because her friends know about the affair, and feels constantly humiliated by thoughts of her family's shameful behavior. This constant stress has dramatically reduced her emotional and physical resilience. Her window of tolerance for painful emotion has constricted and, as far as she's concerned, this is the worst time of her life. Her shame/humiliation/rage cycle involves attacking Michael and Alfred, and confiding in John. Her voice drips sarcasm.) "We're great. Michael still seeing that tramp every day in his classes, and Alfred's lawyer says he might get off with community service for shoplifting, though we still don't know if he's stopped drinking and using drugs. Everything's wonderful."

Alfred: "I can't go anywhere. How am I going to get high anyway?"

Judith: (She notices the rest of the family recoil as Jennifer talks.) "How's everyone else doing?"

John: (His role of being the good one in the family has been sorely tested the last few months. Alfred has always teased him mercilessly, and his mother has increasingly used him as a confidant for the last two years as she's drifted apart from Michael, which often leaves him feeling ashamed and inadequate since he really doesn't know how to help other than to listen and agree with her. John knows way more than he'd like about the affair, his parent's marriage, and Alfred's legal and substance abuse problems. He still tries to keep things normal.) "OK, I guess."

Alfred: (At this point he instinctively creates tension whenever there's an opportunity. In a family where there are strict, rigid moral standards, a difficult child can reflexively break rules, often partly because he feels how the rigid should-patterns are somehow unhealthy and need to be challenged.) "In your dreams. Mom's going crazy, and Dad's getting it on the side."

Michael: (Roused out of his passivity by this embarrassing display, he snaps at Alfred.) "Watch your mouth."

Alfred: "Well, you are, aren't you?"

Michael: (Speaking stiffly.) "I've stopped seeing Sally." (Jennifer winces at the sound of Sally's name.) "I made a mistake and now I'm trying to make it right."

Jennifer: "That's *so* romantic, Michael. You stop screwing your twenty year old graduate student to try to make it right with your old hag wife."

Michael: (Taking her bait, he responds passive-aggressively by focusing on the facts of her statement rather than her pain at betrayal and yearning to be claimed as his lover.) "Come on, Jennifer, she's twenty-seven."

Jennifer: "*Excuse* me."

Judith: "I can see how angry and ashamed you all are."

Alfred: "I'm not ashamed of anything."

Jennifer: "That's not what you said to the police." (This scores. Alfred respects cops, and the contempt that the arresting officer directed toward him hurt.)

Alfred: (Now speaking more authentically to his mother.) "I said I was sorry, and I am. I haven't smoked any pot since I was arrested, and I haven't drunk anything."

Jennifer: (Not wanting to give up her option to attack and demean for relief, she contemptuously discounts his genuine efforts to improve.) "That's because we're drug testing you twice a week. Would you be so squeaky-clean if we weren't checking up on you?" (Alfred hangs his head.)

Judith: (She notices John's depressed expression. *"He has the most credibility in the family right now. If I could open him up, maybe that would create some opportunity for real contact."*) "John, what do you think everyone should do? I think the family respects your opinion."

Alfred: "Yeah, John's perfect."

Judith: (She notices how Jennifer and Alfred express their anger with sarcasm and demeaning attacks. *"It's too soon to point it out. They'd both get over-whelmed by the idea that they hurt others for relief, and Jennifer couldn't tolerate that Alfred has modeled himself emotionally after her."* Speaking to Alfred.) "You sound angry. Tell John what you resent." (Alfred looks down and mumbles something about how John can say what he wants. He vaguely knows he put his brother down unfairly and is ashamed. Judith attunes to him, looks him in the eyes with understanding and care, and thus helps reg-ulate him to a more functional level of arousal.) "I'm serious, Alfred. Anger is just an emotion that usually includes impulses to attack. You can tell John what makes you mad without attacking."

Alfred: (Speaking to John.) "You always do what they want. You follow all the rules, and that makes me look like the bad one."

John: "I'm just trying to do what I'm supposed to. I don't like it when you get in trouble. I don't like it that you're on me so much. What did I ever do to you?"

Alfred: (His face suddenly feels hot.) "I don't mean anything. It's just the way I am."

Judith: (She wants to introduce the idea that value systems and people's sto-ries about their lives can change with new perspectives. She has an intuition that John, who steers clear of conflict but obviously is tuned into everyone, has some valuable insights.) "John, I'd like you to tell your parents and your brother what you believe about the current problems."

John: (He feels safe with Judith, and the idea of just speaking his mind is a relief. He surrenders and pours it out, though he still can't talk to his family directly, or look them in the eyes as he speaks.) "I think Mom and Dad should stop fighting about Sally, or get a divorce. Alfred's smart but doesn't try in school. His friends are losers, and he'll end up in jail if he can't change." (Michael looks respectful, Jennifer's lip is quivering and she seems on the edge of another outburst, and Alfred looks down.)

Judith: (She notices how John instinctively leaves his own interests out of his statement, and feels a wave of compassion and affection for his struggles. *"I'll bet your job is to never be a problem and not need anything."*) "I'd like you to tell your family what you need."

John: (This question genuinely confuses him. Just the idea of talking about what he needs seems wrong somehow. He looks away.) "I'm fine. What I need isn't important."

Here is a family in the first stages of confronting their shame. Morally, both boys have passed from the five to eleven conformist stage of development where the rules are sacred, into the more flexible rational stage where they can sometimes evaluate the relative truth or falseness of facts and perspectives.[18] Like most teens they are contemptuous of hypocrisy, and particularly of the hypocrisy of advocating one set of rules and living by another. Their father's infidelity and their mother's vicious sarcasm are at odds with the values they've always preached, and the boys are repulsed by this (and ashamed of it because we tend to identify with family members) without knowing exactly why. Contemptuous moral condemnation is a form of punishment, a sense of righting a disturbing transgression by condemning the offender. This is a common form of moral thinking for younger children and especially boys, and for people in general when they, like Jennifer, are in defensive states of amplified or numbed emotion, distorted perspectives, destructive impulses, reduced empathy, and limited ability to self-reflect. Teen contempt has the added element of viewing parents as ineffectual and weak, which is particularly provocative to parents and tends to hook their defensive reflexes.

Developmentally, Michael is relatively mature intellectually, and immature interpersonally. Since interpersonal and psychosexual development, or self-reflection in most forms, were alien concepts during his upbringing, his reactions to emotional and interpersonal pain are egocentric and primitive. The increasing arguments and putdowns with Jennifer the last two years have resulted in him telling himself the story that she's not interested or respectful of him as a man, and that it makes sense to get his needs met elsewhere. Sally first saw him last year while he was lecturing passionately about the mathematics of complexity theory. His professional persona of being knowledgeable, confident, present, and passionate presented a resolved masculine person that was intensely attractive to her. Because of her own needs to be viewed as special, she cultivated and amplified her sexual attraction for him, flirted openly in class, and participated enthusiastically when he wanted to pursue a secret affair. It's been hard for her these last few weeks to not see him intimately, and she'll cause further negative drama in the months to come by complaining to the Department Chair, calling Jennifer, and begging Michael to take her back. Like most men who begin affairs caught up in adolescent fantasies, Michael will eventually be shocked and horrified at the scope of collateral damage that is ultimately generated for lots of people by his decision to cheat on his wife.

Jennifer is a pluralistic, egalitarian woman who experiences herself as respecting lots of perspectives, but is unconsciously offended when someone disagrees with her. Like most women, she grew morally from selfish, to caring, to caring for everyone but, since it was never acceptable for her to be angry in her family of origin, she developed no skills in that area, and when she gets mad she simultaneously denies it, blames others, and self-righteously attacks for relief. In addition to the discriminative jealousy she feels for Michael's affair, her personal story of her family being perfect and she being a paragon of wife, mother, church activist, and community member has been shattered by his relationship with Sally and by Alfred's troubles. Under the influence of these stressors she unconsciously tells herself the story that her impeccable character and perfect life have been sabotaged by her selfish husband and son, and she unconsciously is trying to get them to regulate her shame and rage by humiliating them into somehow taking the blame and responsibility for all the problems. The idea that her marriage and her family are systems that she and Michael have cocreated (and are both responsible for) is currently outrageous and unacceptable to her. It would be too shameful for her to believe that these ugly problems have anything to do with her demanding perfectionism and conflicted eroticism. Judith will have to move slowly and lovingly to help her become aware of her defensive viciousness and develop more mature capacities to love herself, her husband, and her children.

What Judith is doing in this third session is attuning to each individual and the family as a system. She is holding the group together in her office with her caring, empathy, and authority, and gradually encouraging everyone to self-reflect on their emotions, their internal representations, and their moment-to-moment relationships with each other. She is helping them begin to feel, tolerate, and observe their shame, humiliation, rage, yearning, and love, and consider using these experiences to change their behavior and internal representations.

Shame begins as a social emotion, and the shame family of emotions is particularly prominent in relational conflict and psychotherapy. Since most of us have learned to organize our lives to avoid awareness of, or responsibility for, these feelings, much of therapy is helping people examine them in a safe environment and use their discoveries to change destructive behaviors and unrealistic, primitive should-patterns. The following is an excerpt from their twenty-fifth session:

Judith: (Everyone comes in joking with each other.) "You guys look happy today."

Jennifer: "Michael got permanent tenure yesterday."

Alfred: "That means we don't have to move."

Jennifer: "It means more than that, Al. It means your father has gotten the recognition he deserves for his work on complex systems."

Judith: "You sound proud of Michael."

Jennifer: "I am. He's worked hard for this." (He looks embarrassed.) "You have, darling, in more ways than one."

Judith: "Tell him what you mean."

Jennifer: "You know, Michael. It was so bad with you and Sally; the Chair reprimanding you and all the problems we've had. It made it more difficult for your work to shine. It's still hard. I get so mad and humiliated sometimes. I wish that woman would get her Ph.D. and take the first bus out of town." (Alfred and John laugh. Jennifer laughs a little too.) "You laugh, boys, but it will be a relief."

Michael: (He responds with his feelings without being cued by Judith, which is huge progress for him.) "Thank-you, sweetheart. It feels good to have you on my side. You've been great. When you were so angry, I was afraid you'd get sick."

Jennifer: "Well, that's one thing I've learned from all this; when I get mad I want to blame somebody and hurt them. That still seems ugly to me."

Judith: "The feelings and the impulses are not ugly. They are just feelings and impulses that are there to inform and guide us. You using them to love your family better is beautiful." (She notices John smile, and smiles back.) "What's on your mind?"

John: (Still embarrassed talking about himself, John blushes. He's learned to attend to his thoughts and feelings and express them in the therapy session, so he plows ahead, albeit somewhat awkwardly.) "Nothing, uh, I just like it when we get along. That's all." (Judith keeps looking at him expectantly, and so he continues, this time to his parents.) "I was worried that you guys would get a divorce, and that Al would end up in jail."

Alfred: (He has the arrogant confidence of a substance abusing teenager who has been sober for eight months and believes he knows everything and can do anything.) "You just wanted me gone so you could have our room to yourself." (John throws a tissue box at his brother, and Michael tells them to cool it.)

Judith: "Is it that hard to admit that you and your brother love each other?" (Now Alfred is embarrassed. It's shameful to him to publicly acknowledge love. His internal representation of himself has been that he's too cynical and worldly to openly talk about loving someone. This has been slowly changing in therapy, but it will be years before he can look another person in the eye and say, "I love you," without embarrassment.) "Yeah, all right. You're a good brother, John, and you've helped me with my program."

The difference in this family is that everyone has learned how to better identify and tolerate their feelings, and there is an emerging understanding in each member of new responsibilities to care for themselves and others. Developmentally this means that rather than becoming overwhelmed by feelings and cycling into immature defensive states they have more tolerance for awareness of their feelings, more tolerance for the presence of previously unacceptable emotions such as shame, rage, and explicit love, and more skills and resolve for using them to enhance intimacy and support growth.

We all grow on many different lines of development with the "include and transcend" rhythm we talked about earlier. Morally, boys grow from selfish (mostly one to four), to respecting rights of group members (five to eleven), to respecting rights for everyone (teen years and beyond). Girls grow from selfish, to caring for group members, to caring for everyone.[19] Interpersonally, we grow from egocentric, to wanting to conform relationally with the cultures we value, to yearning for deeper intimacies that involve more self-acceptance and transparent sharing.[20] With shame, we grow from feeling it in the presence of other's disapproval and needing others to help us regulate it, to being additionally able to disapprove of ourselves and developing immature methods of avoiding, distracting, or ignoring, to using shame as a guide to create health, emotional/spiritual/moral growth, and intimacy. Some developmental lines, like playing the piano, or doing math, can be relatively independent of other developmental lines. Most are interwoven together like strands of a rope. I believe the line of our ability to consciously sense and effectively process the shame feelings is an important strand in many lines of development including moral, psychosexual, interpersonal, values, cognitive, spiritual, and our self-line (the sense of who it is that is looking out from behind our eyes). The more self-aware and accomplished we are at dealing with shame emotions, the more effectively we can adjust our behaviors and our internal representations (our should-patterns), thus enhancing our health and supporting our development on many other developmental lines.

1. Hawkins (2000)

2. Wilber (2006)

3. Deida (1995, 1997, 2004)

4. Siegal (2005)

5. Wilber (2003)

6. Siegal (2005)

7. Enard and Paabo (2004), Lemonick (2006)

8. Wilber (2000)

9. Cloniger (2004), Siegal (2005)

10. Siegal (2005)

11. Brizendine (2006)

12. Schore (2003)

13. Ibid

14. Siegal (1999), Schore (2003)

15. Nathanson (1987)

16. Schore (2003)

17. Siegal (2005)

18. Wilber (2000)

19. Gilligan (1993)

20. Wilber (2000)

4

Shame and Consciousness

From *Lullaby*

I love you when the world is brown
I love you when it is blue
I love you humongous big
I love you tinty little too.
I love you into the clouds
Way up past the starry veil
To the edge of the universe
Beyond, for better or for worse

I love you when it is small
Past the atom's particles
Into the heart of a cosmic string
A universe with stars and things
To a sun, lots of lovely worlds
Music comes from the third of which
A garden place all blue and green
Through a window straight to you and me

It is what it is
Om
It is what it is

I believe consciousness exists within a multidimensional, fluid, interior amalgam of relationships between multiple aspects ourselves, constantly relating with the people, objects, and other sensory inputs from the environment, and with multiple aspects of our past, present, and future. This is not a simile (as in "consciousness is *like* multiple relationships"), or a statement that relating is what consciousness does. Consciousness exists *within* these multiple relationships; it is *interior* to them.

As we explored in Chapter Three, about two hundred thousand years ago, there was a slight change in the human genome that has had staggering effects on every aspect of the Earth's ecosystem. Out of 715 pairs on the FOXP2 gene, there was a stable mutation on two pairs, enabling humans to engage in symbolic communication. None of the other five hominid groups have this mutation, and all humans do, empowering us to abstract aspects of our experience and environment into interior symbols and concepts, and express them as language to others *and ourselves*. I believe that this capacity for symbolic communication combined with memory and awareness of past, present, and future resulted in the infinite progression of communication systems with others and ourselves, within which resides human consciousness.

Our capacities for language, memory, and anticipation are crucial aspects of consciousness-within-multiple-relationships. The reflexive creation of implicit invariant representations starts in the womb, and many believe that the oceanic feelings of oneness and bliss that can spontaneously arise in waking, dreaming, or deep sleep, or be learned and strengthened with contemplative practices, involves neural networks first constellated in the womb.[1] Brains scan, record, and anticipate, gradually developing hierarchies of responses to different perceptual, emotional, and behavioral cues. Our instinct to scan the environment and match it with what we anticipate is radically accelerated as we begin to develop explicit memory as toddlers. Explicit memory involves focal attention, or will, and incorporates a sense of the past, present, and future. Apes have parallel development with humans *until the advent of explicit memory and language*. At that point relative human development on most lines takes off like a rocket. The human capacities for language, explicit memory, self-awareness (one part of me being consciously in relation to another part of me), and approval/disapproval combine to create a series of interior and external relational transformations that lead us from undifferentiated cells to *consciousness,* which involves the capacity for conscious identification with everything. As Ken Wilber and numerous developmentalists have established, personal evolution on all developmental lines has direction, with each new wave including and transcending previous ones. The progression, absent trauma, is always in one direction, towards wider embrace, more complexity, and a deeper sense of felt spirituality. Children are born selfish and become more caring, we crawl before we walk, and we think magically before we can think rationally. In terms of the development of our "self", the evolutionary direction is *from* undifferentiated cells *through* consciousness (a mystery that exists *interior to* our multidimensional interior amalgam of relationships) *towards* conscious identification with everything (the deeper we develop our "self" line, the wider our caring for and identification with larger groups of people, beings, and objects). Let's examine this progression of relationships from an atomic level through some of the include-and-transcend waves of human development:

- All atoms and subatomic particles are infused with energies that interact (relate) with each other. Cosmic strings are multidimensional energetic constructs, interacting to produce subatomic particles, interacting to produce atoms.

- A single hydrogen atom in space relates with gravitational sources and with the mysterious force that is influencing the universe to constantly expand.

- Gravity pulls atoms together in space to form suns, elements, and planets.

- Elements combine to form compounds, which interact in energetically charged environments to form amino acids and other carbon compounds.

- Amino acids, chemicals, water, and energy combine to form primitive life forms a half billion years ago in the ancient oceans of Earth.

- All living organisms have capacities to perceive, reproduce, and interact physically and energetically with similar and different organisms. An amoeba bounces into another amoeba and interacts differently than if it bounces into a paramecium. A virus responds differently to different forms of cells it encounters.

- Creatures with nervous systems have the added capacities to perceive the environment and respond in more complicated ways. Go scuba diving and reach for a lobster, and the lobster will try to evade your grasp.

- Mammals' brains have the added capacities to learn from experience, care about family members, and pass knowledge on to their young. Mothers tend their offspring, teach by approving and disapproving through non-verbal signals, and groups cooperate to some extent for survival, communicating to each other through movement, touch, smell, and sound.

- Some mammals, particularly humans and the great apes, have the added linguistic capacity to manipulate images, symbols, and concepts.

- Humans have the additional capacities to perceive a past, present, and future, to inhabit multiple perspectives, to conceive of their own deaths, and to communicate symbols and concepts with each other *and themselves* through speech, writing, images, music, movement, poetry, mathematics, and countless other forms of interior and external expression.

- Each of these progressive capacities has characteristic energetic qualities that can be observed, measured, and subjectively experienced. These energies are *interobjective* in that science can observe many of them interacting, and *intersubjective* in that we can feel many of the qualitative shifts in relation to ourselves and others.[2]

This relational progression reflects the include-and-transcend nature of evolution and development in species and individuals. As you can see, moving from atoms to consciousness, there is a widening scope of capacities for relating. When a being hits the relational level of capacity for symbolic communication with self and others combined with memory of past, present, and future ... bingo: consciousness.

What do you mean by "within a multidimensional relational construct?"

Sometime during the second trimester a child's implicit memory begins to create invariant representations. Six months after birth an infant discovers she is separate physically from the universe, and around a year old discovers she is emotionally separate from caregivers. These are early steps on the road to conscious self-awareness. Approval and disapproval from others (especially care-givers) affects babies' nervous systems in the ways we've already explored.

Children create internal representations of caregivers. An internal representation of an approving/disapproving, caring/absent parental presence stimulates analogous internal relationships that become increasingly elaborated throughout life.[3] Sigmund Freud's id, ego, and superego[4], Carl Jung's archetypes[5] and complexes, Fritz Perls' introjects[6], and cognitive scientists' schema[7] are all perspectives of internal representations and their elaborations. At eighteen months a child develops the capacity for explicit memory, which first involves the ability to consciously remember information not based in time (for example, bananas taste good) and soon after includes the ability to remember incidents anchored in time (for instance, yesterday I stayed in the sun too long and got sunburned). The capacity for memory comes fully on line around five, which explains why most of us have only sporadic early memories. Throughout this process, the child is creating meaning. Robert Kegan, author of *The Evolving Self*, believes that the instinct to create meaning is a central force in development. Meaning involves the stories we tell ourselves to explain us, others, and the world. We have numerous areas of creating meaning (most of which are aligned with developmental lines), all involving internal representations of how we believe we are supposed to be compared with how we experience ourselves in the present moment (or currently imagine ourselves in the past or future). These areas of meaning include morality, sexuality, social relationships, our physical body, power or position on social hierarchies, our identity as a man or woman, what we value, our professional identities, and many more. All contribute to various aspects of our auto-biographical narratives; the stories we tell ourselves about our lives (another internal relational process; the stories we tell ourselves about our lives).

Our stories mature as we mature. Young children inhabit primarily magical stories (I can magically make Mommy appear by thinking about her). Elementary schoolers grow to mythic stories where external sources of authority like parents, ministers, teachers, and sacred books, have special powers. Teens and adults tend to tell themselves rational stories that make logical sense. College culture tends to support stories that are multicultural, egalitarian, and non-hierarchical. If people continue to grow, they tend to tell more integrally informed stories that involve pleasure in multiple points of view, and reduced fear of death and the world in general. Each of these types of stories has an ethical/moral infrastructure, which reflects the internal representations of how we should be.[9] Here is where shame can appear at any level as our behaviors, thoughts, and impulses, don't jive with our, or other's, should-systems. *Every level of relating has the potential for approval/ disapproval from self and/or others. Where there is disapproval, there is potential for shame emotions.*

When we remember a past action, *we are relating to ourselves* in the past. When we anticipate a future action, *we are relating to ourselves* in the future. As we develop language, the capacity to internally hold and manipulate images, symbols, and concepts and express them to others, *we are relating to others.* When we think in images, symbols, or concepts (literally speaking internally to ourselves), *we are relating to ourselves.* As we automatically scan our external and internal environments, comparing what we perceive to our internal representations, *we are relating to our internal representations*, and often reflexively adjusting them in response to new experiences, *sometimes with conscious intent.* According to Jeff Hawkins (and I agree with him), most of these adjustments are done automatically. On the other hand, perception, memory, and cognition are all affected and directed by conscious attention. Self-awareness involves one part of us being aware of another part of us, self-reflection one part of us considering another part of us, and self-evaluation one part of us judging another part of us; all forms of relating. Thus all manifestations of consciousness (short of complete non-dual awareness where there is only unity) have internal or external relating components.

Humans relate from multiple perspectives with approval or disapproval.

Maturation on most developmental lines involves deepening consciousness, which often involves more caring and just perspectives seeming progressively more beautiful, good, and true. Since development is include and transcend, we don't completely loose old habits as we grow into new worldviews; rather we integrate them into more complex networks that add *preferable* new choices and perspectives to previous ones. The breadth of human ability to take multiple perspectives is mind-blowing. My dog can chew up shoes, and feel ashamed when I communicate disapproval through expression, tone, gesture, and "No!" My dog cannot imagine me thinking about my friend Kevin looking at his son Dean being ashamed because he wrecked Kevin's car. Only humans can occupy these multiple perspectives that involve awareness of actions and consequences from different viewpoints in past, present, and future. This is reflected in every creation myth, where humans are distinguished from animals in that they have a conscious choice as to whether they eat the apple, defy the Gods, or enter the new land. People in these stories are blessed with the potential for awareness of consequences from the perspectives of themselves, others, and the Gods.

Since emotions saturate all experience, there are emotional components inherent in every perspective. In the midst of all our relating and automatic comparisons of experience with internal representations, we are attracted or repulsed, excited or innervated, interested or bored, frightened or reassured, approving or disapproving. Any disapproval we have for ourselves, whether in perceiving another's criticism, or experiencing our own negative reaction for not conforming with an internal should-system, potentially can evoke a shame emotion.

Shame and consciousness.

Practically, the relationship of shame and consciousness has staggering consequences to our development and the subjective fabric of our lives because we can't self-regulate shame in a mature way until at least our teen years when we finally have the brain capacity to consistently inhabit "what if?" scenarios, and hold opposing concepts simultaneously. For example, I might feel ashamed that I failed a test, but the teacher told us to study the wrong chapter, and so I need to adjust my should-system to not feel ashamed when I've been misinformed, but also to care for (instead of angrily humiliate) the one who misinformed me. Until we've developed this mature capacity and have been trained in using it to examine shame and adjust either our behavior or our should-system, we'll instinctively respond to shame emotions with seeking out an important person to look at us with approval, complying with the should-standard we believe we've violated, or trying to avoid the shame experience with strategies like rage, blaming others, seeking stimulation, suppression, repression, projection, distraction, or scapegoating.

Arguably there is an approval/disapproval aspect to most human experience. Plato and numerous subsequent philosophers have observed that humans evaluate the world from the objective concrete observable (the true), the subjective individual aesthetic (the beautiful), and the collective subjective moral (the good). Some modern scientists seem to struggle to stay aloof from the beautiful and good standards; maintaining that science only deals with the empirically verifiable true. As a result, the shame emotions tend to create confused judgments when they inevitably show up. A recent study showing boys and girls benefiting from same-sex teachers in same-sex classes drew scathing reviews, none of them scientifically based, all of them disapproving, with nobody really examining the shame emotions that were being evoked by this unpopular finding.[10]

We can feel shame from any perspective.

There are multiple possible shame perspectives in the above example with Dean wrecking Kevin's car. Kevin could feel ashamed that his son wrecked the car, or Dean could feel ashamed that his dad is ashamed. In future years, Kevin could observe my son Ethan denting his car, which might cause him to remember Dean wrecking his car, which could stimulate shame. I could feel embarrassed observing Kevin watching a movie of someone wrecking a car. From any of these perspectives, our habits, our hierarchies of primed responses, are to deal with shame in the ways we learned as children.

Without the ability to bring mature caring attention to the shame emotions, any aspect of human consciousness is likely to be affected in surprising ways. For example, the paradox of social conservatives emphasizing personal freedom (anti-tax, anti-gun control, and anti-government regulation) and legislating moral restrictions (the twentieth century sodomy laws in the southern states, restricted access to birth control and sex education, and proposed flag burning and anti-homosexual constitutional amendments) seems to reflect an avoidance of self-reflection on the shame emotions that might be motivating apparently contradictory positions.

Will, consciousness, and ever widening circles of perspectives and relationships.

If our consciousness exists interior to an ocean of internal relationships, what characterizes it from other aspects of mind? Memory, perception, behavioral priming, intuition, and relationship with self and others in past/present/future can all be both conscious and unconscious. What seems unique to consciousness is *will*. I can consciously will my thought, attention, body, and behavior in different directions. I can do this in full harmony with habit or behavioral priming (as when I reach for the apple when hungry), or completely against habit or behavioral priming (as when I leap out of an airplane on my first solo skydiving adventure). Conscious will is how we navigate the infinite possibilities of existence. Conscious will is how we can move a low probability behavior (like self-reflecting on shame) higher on our response hierarchies. Conscious will, utilized consistently over time, can shape our perspectives, our behaviors, our development, and our actual brain structures[11] by empowering us to evoke specific states of consciousness that are reinforced each time we inhabit them; eventually stabilizing as hard-wired neural networks. If consciousness is a mysterious entity that is interior to our infinity of internal relationships, will is the force that directs and guides. How we choose to think and behave will be influenced by our internal representations of who we are and believe we should be, but our will has the last word. If we cultivate self-reflection, satisfaction at being consistent with should-patterns and shame at not living up to those patterns can guide us to utilize will to navigate our lives towards optimal health, growth, and caring.

We are conceived as multicellular organisms, begin implicit learning in utero, and by seven months of age differentiate physically from the universe, thus creating self and other. We then go through progressive include-and-transcend stages of differentiating emotionally from parents, developing explicit memory, relating to others and ourselves in the past, present, and future through progressive worldviews, identifying with and relating to wider ranges of external and internal figures, and ultimately moving toward identifying, this time through depth and knowledge rather than immaturity and innocence, with everything that's arising. This whole process of expanding consciousness is interior to a multidimensional *intra*personal and *inter*personal relational system that is drenched with approval and disapproval, and thus shame and the shame family of emotions. Since shame tends to block clear examination, it is potentially a major stumbling block on our developmental path. Since shame leads us to discrepancies between our perceptions of ourselves and our should-patterns, it is potentially a major guide to development. When we have the will to tolerate shame, accept it, feel through it to differentiate the behaviors and should-patterns involved, and appropriately process them to feel a subjective sense of unity, shame is transformed to harmonious integration. This is how we can use shame to grow from alienation to transcendence.

Here is sixteen-year-old Teresa coming home at eleven (her curfew is 10:30) with her boyfriend Preston who, in seven years, will become her first husband. She and her family settled down in a suburb of Washington D.C. when Teresa was fourteen. Teresa blossomed in high school as an outstanding student and song-leader. For the past hour, she and Preston have been necking in his car. Both are in emotionally/erotically aroused states (which tend to make us more reckless[12]). Preston walks Teresa to the door, and Pam, with Stewart in the background, opens it as they step onto the porch. The mood is tense:

> Pam: (The sight of Teresa in her revealing summer dress cues memories of her own adolescence. *"I had a cute figure too when I was sixteen, but my mother would never have allowed that hemline. It's so unfair."* Riding this bubble of resentment, she confronts the young couple.) "You're thirty minutes late."

> Teresa: (She blushes and looks down, embarrassed by the yucky scene and especially by her mother smelling of alcohol. *"Why can't you be nice?"*) "The movie lasted longer than we thought."

> Pam: "Come on, the movie was over hours ago. Preston, you should know better."

> Preston: (He's a good student, the star guard on the school basketball team, and feels entitled to do what he wants. On the other hand, he likes Teresa's family, is crazy about Teresa, and is somewhat embarrassed at spending the last hour kissing and fondling Pam's daughter. He responds to his embarrassment with compliance.) "You're right, I'm sorry. It's not Teresa's fault, we were having so much fun that I lost track of time."

> Stewart: (Preston taking full responsibility is attractive to him. His internal representation of a good man is one who takes as much on himself as possible, and it seems honorable to distort reality to protect a woman. This is the kind of young man he's valued and led in the military for over twenty years. *"I like this kid."*) "That's OK son, just don't do it again."

Preston: (He's a little in awe of a Navy captain, and he loves the approving tone.) "Thank-you, sir. I'll do better next time." (Teresa, happily off the hook, gives him a chaste kiss on the cheek and runs inside, thinking, *"I can't wait till I'm away at college."*)

Pam: (She smiles in spite of herself, knowing Teresa wouldn't stay out past curfew if she didn't want to. This has unexpectedly turned into a warm scene. *"They're just teenagers, and Preston is so cute."*) "Nice seeing you Preston." (As he walks to his car and she closes the door, she responds to her embarrassment at being attracted to Preston by angrily remembering waiting thirty minutes past curfew for Teresa, and so she attacks Stewart.) "You know he was bullshitting."

Stewart: (He looks at Pam with distaste. She's aged badly in the last ten years, and is drunk and angry most nights. *"You've let yourself go, drinking and eating. I wish I could look at you the way Preston looks at Teresa. I'd leave you in a minute if it wasn't for the children."*) "Ease up, Pam. They're only a little late, and Preston's a good student and athlete. You're way too hard on her. What do you want?" (She flushes at his rebuke, and he feels some pleasure at hurting her, and then guilty for being cruel. His internal representation of a good man is one who is never disrespectful to women.)

Pam: "I want you to not be such a dummy." (She feels satisfaction at the look of angry humiliation on Stewart's face, then remorse for her nasty attack, and then quickly more self-righteous anger. They go to bed tense and unfulfilled, as they have countless nights before.)

In three years, when Teresa is away on scholarship to the University of California at Santa Barbara, Stewart will divorce Pam. Their marital conflict and lack of loving contact will be amplified with Teresa, the family balancer and peacemaker, away at college. At this point the marriage is coasting with Stewart and Pam leading increasingly parallel lives while regularly engaging in pointless arguments to avoid the anger and shame they feel over their inability to be true to their internal representations of good husband/wife. The lack of love feels wrong to both, and each blames the other for it.

Since Teresa has discovered that she's smart and cute, she's been living as much of her life as she can at school and with friends. The last six months she's been intoxicated with Preston, her first serious boyfriend who will join her at college in Santa Barbara. They will break up the first year because he insists on dating other girls, and then they'll reconnect senior year, live together, and marry at twenty-four.

Consciousness and will is revealed in all the intrapersonal and interpersonal relating in the above episode, through past, present, and future. The internal and external dialogs only give the surface flavor of the myriad aspects of each person relating to thoughts, feelings, sensations, memories, anticipations, and perceptions in themselves and others. Internal representations intrude into consciousness as memories, and associations are cued. Consciousness alters internal representations as new experiences occur. Approval and disapproval of self and others permeate each aspect of the episode. Will directs thought and behavior in selfish, caring, rational, and irrational directions with varying degrees of conscious awareness or consistent purpose. *Rarely is shame processed.* To a certain extent, everyone is engaged in an elaborate social dance partially designed to avoid shameful thoughts, feelings, behaviors, and memories. The power of each person's will to choose caring and mature perspectives and actions is diluted by habit, avoidance, and resistance to self-awareness of uncomfortable truths.

Contrast the above dialog to the following excerpt from the forty-fifth therapy session with John and his family in Santa Barbara. At this point John is seventeen and has already been accepted into U.C. Santa Barbara, where he'll date Teresa during the years she and Preston are broken up. They'll meet again in their thirties, fall in love, and proceed to create the relationship we observed in Chapter One. He and his family have been in therapy now for over two years, and the culture of the session finds self-reflection beautiful and good:

Judith: "I haven't seen your family in five weeks. What brings us together?"

Jennifer: "Alfred has been cutting school to be with his girlfriend." (John and Michael can't help laughing at this, and Jennifer blushes.) "You guys go ahead and have your laugh. I'm worried. You know what kids do when they're alone and unsupervised."

Michael: "I'm worried too, but he's been doing well at school, and we like Mary."

Alfred: (He's embarrassed, but looks right at his parents and responds.) "I know what you're thinking, but we know we're too young to, you know, go all the way. Besides she a good Catholic girl."

Judith: (Raised Catholic, she laughs involuntarily.) "I'm sorry, I shouldn't laugh. I was brought up Catholic, and some of us were a little loose with the rules." (Seeing smiles and raised eyebrows all around, she blushes.)

John: "You're blushing, Judith."

Judith: "I guess we all have some emotional charge around sexual material."

Alfred: "Mom, you're right I shouldn't be cutting classes. There was a huge west swell, and Mary said she'd drive us to Rincon."

Michael: "You could have surfed after school, son. Besides, won't it cause trouble with Mary's family that she helped you cut school?"

Alfred: "You're not going to tell them, are you?"

Judith: "What do you think is best, Alfred?" (He shakes his head, temporarily inarticulate with mortification.)

John: (He's grown to respect Alfred as a fun companion and superior surfer, and is drawn to help his brother.) "I don't think it will be that bad. You weren't having sex, you were surfing. Just tell them you won't do it anymore, and then don't do it."

Michael: "That's good advice, Al. I'm a parent, and I respect it when a kid admits a mistake, says they'll improve, and follows through. We all make mistakes." (He exchanges a glance with Jennifer, who gives him a reassuring smile. Their relationship has benefited from the new openness and honesty that has resulted from processing his affair.)

Alfred: (*"I hate it, but they're right. I'll call tonight and get it over with; no, better still, I'll go over and talk to Mary and then her parents."*) "OK, you guys. I'll go over to Mary's tonight and talk to her parents." (He sees approval on everyone's face and is suddenly proud. *"It's the right thing to do."*)

Consciousness and will are manifested very differently here than they are in the episode with Teresa, Preston, Pam, and Stewart. The culture of this session supports feeling, acknowledging, and processing shame emotions with the goal of serving the highest good. As a result, everyone is clearer, more self-accepting, more accepting of others, and more able to will themselves toward changing behaviors and internal representations. Jennifer went from feeling ashamed of Alfred to feeling proud of him. Alfred shifted from it being completely inconsistent with his internal representation of himself to have the talk with Mary and her family, to having an internal representation of himself being the kind of guy who could have a mature dialog about an embarrassing subject. How we use our will to feel and process shame has huge consequences to our experience of, and continuing development of, consciousness. Within the infinite perspectives available to each of us, there are optimal ways of internal and external relating, just as there are optimal states of consciousness to best open each moment. Consciousness floats in these infinite perspectives, guided by our internal representations, our will, and our habits. The more we use our will to guide us to self-reflection, compassionate understanding, superior perspectives, and right action, the more harmonious our infinity of inner relationships become, and the easier it is to take responsibility for everything we experience and do.

1. Siegal (2005)

2. Wilber (2000)

3. Kernberg (1975), Druck (1989), Masterson (1981)

4. Freud (1949)

5. Jung's (1961)

6. Perls (1968)

7. Gilbert (2002)

8. Kegan (1982)

9. Wilber (2000)

10. Dee (2005), Feller (2006)

11. Siegal (1999)

12. Hutson (2006)

5

Masculine and Feminine

From *Rain Song*

One of them was hungry, searching for a soul
Finding out that love was just a step beyond it all
Iridescent shadows, dancing on the wall
One of them was laughing at the beauty of it all
Here it is, here it is, I love it, yeah
O baby, when you sing me the rain song

Jackie wanted shelter from the teeth of the machine
Bruce had his Harley and some songs about his dreams.
If you were innocent I wouldn't know the difference
Is that your hand? I love it when you make me crazy
Here it is, here it is, I love it, yeah
O baby, when you sing me the rain song

It's ten PM Saturday night and Teresa and Preston are parking three miles out of town by the Old Miller's Pond. The smell of the forest is intoxicating on this beautiful spring evening, and the stars are brilliantly reflected up from the peaceful water. Teresa is seventeen, and they've been going out for fifteen months, a long-term relationship by teen standards. Parking and necking is the final act in a ritual that they've gradually established for weekend nights over the last year. First they party with their friends, usually at someone's house where the parents are gone or comfortably separate in another room. Preston smokes pot and drinks beers with his football buddies while Teresa has one or two wine coolers and giggles with her cheerleading friends. As things begin to get more rowdy, Preston takes Teresa by the hand, leads her to his 66 Mustang, and they drive through the rural farms to a secluded romantic spot like the pond where they kiss and caress until it's time for Teresa to go home. Preston usually presses for more genital touching, and Teresa, though turned on and having fun, resists mildly, establishing the limits of how intimate they can be sexually. So far their level of contact has progressed to mutual masturbation where Preston, and often Teresa, have orgasms, and then he drives her home. Tonight, Preston brought a bottle of Cherry Brandy and is urging Teresa to take a drink:

Preston: "Come on, baby, just try it. It's good." (He takes a swallow.)

Teresa: (She feels safe with Preston who is authoritative and always seems to know what he's doing. On the other hand, it has been an article of faith for her to never get drunk and, unlike most of her friends, she has hardly ever let herself go beyond a mild buzz which she enjoys because a little alcohol usually disinhibits her and seems to make necking more fun.) "OK, if you say." (She takes a tentative swallow. *Kind of like Cherry Coke.*)" "This is good." (Ten minutes later their clothes are scattered on the car seats and the kids are in the back seat, locked in a passionate embrace.)

Preston: (Emboldened by the brandy, he grabs her head and firmly guides it towards his penis. She mumbles a protest, but finds his erotic direction exciting. He speaks in a tender voice.) "You know I love you."

Teresa: (She has never had oral sex before, though the kids refer to it frequently. She inexpertly starts sucking, while he reaches around and caresses her clitoris. Preston has been sexually active for several years, enjoys his partners' pleasure, and is unashamed of "going for it" with Teresa or any other girl he has a sexual opportunity with. Their mutual erotic charge builds quickly until she feels his left hand tighten in her hair, and he has his orgasm, leaving her laughing and sputtering. She's still turned on, and looks up, smiling coyly.) "How was that?"

Preston: "You are the greatest." (They cuddle a little longer and he drives her home.)

The next morning Teresa wakes up hung over and guilty. Even though sex has not been discussed in her house, the "Don't be sexual, especially if you're a girl" message has been omnipresent in her church, school, and family. The teens in her group generally accept the cultural standards, but have their own unspoken rules. Being sexual with your boyfriend is OK if you're intoxicated, don't get pregnant, and don't talk about it much. Cheating on your partner is frowned upon, but the kids eagerly participate in the dramas that ensue when couples break up, are unfaithful, or engage in risky behavior.

Up to this point Teresa has been conservative by her peer standards. She doesn't get drunk, doesn't allow intercourse and, until last night, won't have oral sex. Thinking about the episode while hung over has no erotic appeal, and she is ashamed. She responds to her shame in the most available of the three ways we naturally learn as infants and small children (comply with a rule, get someone to "witness" our shameful behavior and look at us with love and approval, or avoid the painful emotion in some fashion). It's too late to comply with a rule, there's no one available to "witness" (especially in an area like sex that has prohibitions about explicit talk), so she avoids the experience by trying to block it out of her memory, and rationalizing the transgression. *"I got drunk on Cherry Brandy. I won't do that again."*

Preston and Teresa both go on to attend the University of California at Santa Barbara, partly to be together. Preston quickly discovers he can have lots of girls using his charm and sexual skills and feels "trapped" in his relationship with Teresa. They break up after Teresa discovers him cheating for the second time, and she takes it hard, grieving for months and not dating until she meets John who is attentive, safe, sober, and faithful. She naturally feels secure emotionally with John, and senses she can trust him. Their friendship gradually turns into a love affair.

Here is Teresa taking a sunset walk with John on the UCSB beach. They've been lovers for almost a year and intensely enjoy spending time together. "He's really nice, and I can talk to him about everything," is how she describes John to her friends. Sex is a problem, though. They have unsatisfying intercourse once or twice a week (low frequency for college lovers), and Teresa doesn't get that turned on. John doesn't drink, and Teresa follows his lead and generally abstains when with him, which is delightful for many forms of connection, but deprives her of the disinhibiting influence of alcohol that she relied on with Preston to transition into feeling sexy. John is sexually inexperienced and too eager to please. He gets so concerned with his performance that he's anxious in the beginning, and then emotionally disconnected as arousal builds, both of which are usually turn-offs to feminine people like Teresa. On the other hand, he finds her achingly desirable and, walking on the romantic beach next to the campus, all he can think about is how much he wants her:

John: (*"She looks so hot in that blouse. I love her breasts. Don't stare at them you idiot."* He feels a flush of embarrassment, but is still hungry for her.) "Can I kiss you?"

Teresa: (*"I hate it when he asks."*) "Why do you always have to ask?"

John: (Now he's defensive.) "I don't want to kiss you if you don't want to."

Teresa: (This makes sense to her egalitarian feminist principles, which tend to blossom in college students, but there is something repulsive about the whole conversation.) "Well, then no, I don't want to."

John: (Frustrated and irritated. *"She's never interested, and I am so much more mature than most college guys. All they want is sex. I think all of her is great.*) "It doesn't seem fair that I am so much more respectful of you than most guys, and you never seem interested."

Teresa: (Now she feels guilty. *"He's right. He is so sweet, and I'm just not that attracted. I wonder what's wrong with me?"*) "Oh, all right." (She kisses him and they progress into a mild erotic state until John notices some other students walking nearby and, somewhat mortified, stops. Teresa feels the dip in energy.) "What?"

John: "There are people coming." (He grabs her hand and starts walking.)

Teresa: (Strangely, now she feels more powerful and turned on.) "Fuck them, John. Kiss me." (She cuddles into him and kisses him with more passion.)

John: (He likes her energy, but is acutely aware of the laughter and hoots coming from the group of students and responds awkwardly, not realizing how he's selfishly absorbed in his own discomfort and disconnecting from Teresa energetically. *"I wish she wouldn't embarrass me like this."* Sensing his disapproval, Teresa shuts down, stops the kiss, and they continue their walk.)

Five months later they break up, largely because of their inability to have fun erotic contact. A year later, Teresa forgives Preston for cheating on her ("He was just going through an immature college phase," is the story she tells herself), and they get back together. Preston has no problem initiating and enjoying sexual contact with Teresa. They marry at twenty-three and Teresa gives birth to their son Aaron eighteen months later. By the time Aaron is four, Preston has had two affairs.

What's going on here? It seems obvious that John is a more trustable man than Preston, and that any relationship with Preston will end in disaster, and yet Teresa rejects John, marries Preston, and proceeds to have seven years of unhappy, unfaithful relating that will leave her a single mother, struggling to work a job, raise a child, and have a life. When she and John finally meet again, she's thirty-two and in law school, having decided that she can't rely on a man so she has to take care of herself. John, lonely after an amicable divorce from Annie, the woman he married on the rebound from Teresa, feels blessed to find Teresa again. They fall in love, but still have problems with erotic connection until, years later, they eventually develop a passionate erotic polarity through therapy and other emotional/relational work.

What was originally missing for them was an understanding of the principles of masculine/feminine aspects, essence, and erotic polarity, and the abilities to apply those principles is service of love and growth. Part of what blocks many of us from this knowledge is our inability to tolerate and process the shame emotions we have associated with sexual feelings, physiology, behavior, and our own unique combination of masculine and feminine aspects and essence. Let's explore these constructs. As we do, see if you can perceive any tingles of guilt, embarrassment, moral judgment, or shame that you might have in response to the ideas and practices. Noticing, accepting, and reflecting on such reactions often creates opportunities to refine internal representations and adjust perspectives and behaviors to support more passion, growth, and love.

Polarity.

David Deida is a speaker and writer who for years has been teaching the emotional/erotic/spiritual dynamics of life, love, and relationship. He has observed that there is an arc of energy that exists between each of us and anyone or anything we encounter. I walk in a forest and feel a peaceful oneness with nature, I stand by a restaurant and am drawn by the delicious smells, I see a feminine shape and I'm attracted, I hear a piercing train whistle and recoil, or I hold a baby and feel tender and protective. All of these are energetic connections, or polarities.

Erotic polarity is the result of a confluence of a masculine aspect and a feminine aspect. This does not necessarily have to be explicitly sexual. A surfer paddling into a wave, a twelve-year-old girl riding her horse, or a coed adoring her philosophy teacher all involve polarities between masculine (surfer, horse, philosophy teacher), and feminine (ocean, girl, and coed). These masculine/feminine polarities are energetically charged with pleasure, even though the surfer, girl, and coed do not have actual sex (or even conscious erotic sensation) with the ocean, horse, or philosophy professor (well, maybe with the philosophy professor). In lover relationships, how authentically and deeply we inhabit our deepest masculine or feminine sexual essence *and* connect it with love and pleasure to the reciprocal in our lover is a major determinant of the intensity and health of our sexual relationship.[1]

We all have masculine and feminine aspects, but our deepest sexual essence is usually more masculine or feminine.

Each of us exists on a continuum with unchanging pure masculine consciousness on one end, and ever-changing feminine identification and involvement with the world on the other.[2] A wide-open, unconflicted human can inhabit any point on this masculine/feminine continuum if it serves the moment. In deep dreamless sleep, or in profound meditative states, we experience ourselves as one with the unchanging emptiness out of which everything is constantly arising. This is the pure masculine principle. The pure feminine principle is when we are fully in our constantly changing bodies, completely engaged with the countless rich and impermanent objects and processes of the world, relationships, and our senses. All of us have masculine and feminine aspects, but when we are relaxed, open, and fully ourselves we will most often lean more towards either the masculine or the feminine side of the continuum. This is our deepest sexual essence.[3]

People with a more feminine essence tend to delight in the senses, body, community, family, music, color, and masculine presence. People with a more masculine essence tend to delight in deep purpose, meaning at the edge of death, emptiness, being true to principle, solitary spiritual practice, and feminine erotic radiance. Many people say, "But I like all of those things," and it's true, we can find bliss on any point of the masculine/feminine continuum, but what are your responses to the following questions?

- Do you prefer action movies or relationship movies?
- Are you more attracted to the drama of love and betrayal, or meaning at the edge of death (like sports or martial arts)?
- Would you rather go shopping with a good friend, or watch a sporting event where the fate of the season, the title, or a million dollars rests on the outcome?
- Does it sound more blissful to you to sit is austere meditation and lose yourself in the emptiness of the void, or to dance in communion with families, food, color, and music?
- Are you more comfortable in a polished wood room with clean shelves that hold just the books and objects you find most inspiring, or in a color-

ful carpeted room with shelves full of pictures, shells, knick-knacks, and reminders of your friends and family?

Feminine people tend to be attracted to masculine partners who are unrecoiling, true to their principles, confident and fearless, and who are willing and able to know and claim a feminine partner. Feeling known, claimed, safe, and loved by a trustable man is blissful for most women.

Masculine people tend to be attracted to feminine partners who are open channels of emotion, wellsprings of love, and who offer devotional love through their bodies in response to masculine integrity and claim. Feeling an offering of feminine erotic radiance is blissful for most men.

People grow through at least three stages in their masculine and feminine.

Deida suggests that we grow through three broad stages of adulthood, and especially in our sexual relationships. First stage relationships tend to be egocentric, second stage relationships tend to be egalitarian and communication based, and third stage relationships involve opening to serve the highest good in each moment.

In young adulthood we begin our sexual relationships primarily looking to get our needs for recognition, intimacy, sexual release, and status met. First stage feminine people want to be seen and validated as light and love for their own sake, and tend to use their erotic radiance to get their personal needs met. Second stage feminine people downplay sexuality, and are inclined to downplay masculine/feminine differences and believe it is morally superior to be related to in an egalitarian fashion as one equal person to another. Third stage feminine people relax open to their deepest aspects and essences, and surrender to what best serves the moment, usually by expressing emotion through the body, and opening into a full spectrum woman who can be either light or shadow, hard or soft, seductress or divine mother; a wellspring of love.

First stage masculine people want to strive, accomplish, and possess feminine erotic radiance, mostly for their own gratification and gain. Second stage masculine people generally downplay their competitiveness and sexuality, and strive to relate in egalitarian and non-stereotypical ways, using communication skills to achieve fairness in life and relationship. Third stage masculine people source themselves in their deepest purpose and commit to opening the world and their feminine partners. A masculine person in a third stage moment understands that the feminine is the world, and his feminine partner is a concentrated dose of the constantly changing textures of the big feminine (the big She) that is all that changes.

Most of us have first, second, and third stage moments each day. As we grow, we tend to develop from having more first stage moments to having more second and third stage moments. In the classic include-and-transcend rhythm of development, we can shift from having mostly first stage moments, to mostly second stage moments, to mostly third stage moments, depending upon our levels of effort, knowledge, and development. In any moment, *our level of sexual attractiveness is a function of how open we are to our deepest sexual essence, and how effectively we support masculine/feminine polarity with others.*

Shame and erotic polarity.

My son, Ethan, recently called me and breathlessly quoted some statistics from his community psychology class. 35% of college students binge drink at least once a week. 65% of Americans were either addicted to a substance, on a prescription psychotropic drug (usually for depression or anxiety), or have a personality disorder. Studies of many indigenous hunter-gatherer tribes show dramatically fewer of these problems.[4] Something about modern American life creates predictable levels of suffering and pathology.

I'm not romanticizing tribal culture. Individuals from such cultures do badly when transplanted to new milieus (unlike Westerners who are individually much more adaptable) and, in one set of studies, indigenous people were the least altruistic of all the urban, suburban, rural, western, and eastern groups measured for altruism. What tribal cultures often do provide are internal representations for "good" ways of being that individuals can consistently meet, and cultural mechanisms for regulating shame emotions that involve fewer situations where an individual must unilaterally develop avoidance strategies. Hunter-gatherer cultures often provide comprehensive standards that can be met, and supportive social environments that consistently attune with acceptance and approval. Members of such groups rarely worry about "belonging."

Agrarian and industrialized cultures, on the other hand, are rife with standards that can never be met. "Don't be sexual," "Don't feel sexual," "Don't be interested in your or other's genitalia," "Don't make mistakes," "Don't be angry," "Be perfect," "Win or you're worthless," "Follow every rule of 'The Book," and "Don't be interested in forbidden topics," are all common examples of impossible standards. Inability to consistently comply with such rules, and the impossibility of getting approval and loving attention for forbidden thoughts and behaviors (after all, they're forbidden), often leaves children with the third option of avoiding shame emotions (ignoring, distorting, denying, blaming, projecting, suppressing; anything but compassionately feeling, accepting, exploring, and learning). I believe this single mechanism is responsible for an enormous amount of suffering and pathology.

Nowhere are the above processes more evident than is dealing with masculine and feminine aspects/essence, and erotic polarity.

John, Teresa, and Preston through the lens of masculine/feminine aspect, essence, and polarity.

Preston is a classic first stage masculine person relationally. He sees the feminine and wants to penetrate and possess for his own needs. Cruising in his Mustang in high school, or on the prowl at UCSB, he isn't thinking in terms of what serves the highest good, or what serves the women he affiliates with. He sees them, wants them, pursues them, claims them, and betrays them because he wants to and he can. If anyone takes issue with his selfish behavior, his initial reflexive shame quickly turns into anger.

John is a classic second stage masculine person relationally. He desires feminine radiance, but feels guilty at his hunger to ravish and possess, so he suppresses it and focuses on egalitarian, non-hierarchical good communication and fairness. Deida maintains that, "Communication is the religion of the second stage." The idea that Teresa wants him to feel into her and assertively take her erotically when he feels she wants him, and to stand unrecoiling (accepting everything, including shame) if he's wrong, confidently adjusting to her changing moods and desires, feels unfair to him. He wants to communicate so she'll guarantee she won't reject him. Couples' researcher John Gottman has found that *in self-reported good relationships* a bid for attention that isn't met positively is only repeated twenty percent of the time. In bad relationships such bids are hardly ever repeated.[5] This reflects American first and second stage culture. A first stage man won't repeat a rejected overture because, "Why risk rejection? Screw you, I'll find someone else." A second stage man won't repeat a rejected overture because he can't stand the shame of disapproval.

Teresa began relating in high school as a first stage woman. She attracted Preston, the high status athlete, and mostly organized her sexual activity to satisfy her needs. She'd drink to eliminate guilt (her internalized representation was that sexual activity, up to a point, was OK if she was mildly intoxicated), do what pleased her, and feel little responsibility for Preston's growth or fulfillment.

In college Teresa grew into a second stage woman who believed in fairness. Pluralistic academic culture taught her that honest communication was necessary for intimacy, men and women should have equal rights and power, and she should be as independent and successful as any man. Preston's cheating behavior disgusted her, so she broke up and found second stage John who felt safe, but who was unable to ravish her even in the selfish first stage way that Preston had. When she wanted it, being possessed confidently in an authoritative way was blissful. With tepid, second stage John, she felt ashamed of her fantasies of being taken over by a dark powerful masculine presence (fantasies she wasn't safe sharing with anyone until many years later). Since she was a deeply feminine person who yearned to be ravished open, she finally felt compelled to leave.

Third stage relating involves knowing and being true to our deepest sexual essence, feeling into the moment and our partner, and doing our best to open everyone to the deepest passion and spirituality we can. To do so often involves feeling, acknowledging, and processing the shame emotions that we've organized our life to avoid; the fourth option in dealing with shame that is only available to us when our brains are mature enough to inhabit "what if" situations, and we can tolerate pain, look for the internal representations that create and support it, and commit ourselves to changing our behavior to meet our values, and/or our values to meet more compassionate, caring, and realistic standards. Teresa and John's inability to create and sustain satisfying erotic polarity led her to determine that she wasn't "in love" with John. Yearning to be ravished open erotically, she later believes Preston's empty promises of faithfulness and commitment to change in the hope she can be deeply claimed erotically by a trustable man. Like many women, she marries a man for his potential instead of his current abilities.

Teresa doesn't encounter the possibility of third stage relating until, seven years into her marriage, she attends a four-day Gestalt therapy workshop in Esalen, California. By this time her son Aaron is six years old and comfortable spending the week with her father and his new wife. Preston thinks that the new-age Esalen workshops are "airy-fairy," and "wimpy," and refuses to go (though he encourages Teresa because it gives him a week to spend seducing his new secretary). Teresa's college buddy Robin invites her because she loves Teresa, is benefiting enormously herself from the new experiences she is having with the human potential movement, and because she despises Preston (often women friends have a better sense of the integrity of our partners than we do, though it was a slam-dunk evaluation for Robin the first time Preston hit on her). Teresa loves being with Robin and feels intrigued by the ideas of liberation and authenticity that permeate the Esalen catalog.

The two women leave Santa Barbara on a Wednesday afternoon and drive up the California coast into the sunset. The farther north they go, the more beautiful the scenery, and the more separate Teresa feels from her life with Preston. This is the longest time that she's planned away from home since Aaron was born, and there is a delicious sense of freedom in taking a road trip with Robin, something they often enjoyed doing in college. When they arrive at Esalen and spend part of the first evening naked in the baths with men and women they've just met, she is primed for new experiences and awakenings, and sits down the next morning in the workshop circle with eager anticipation.

Fritz Perls, the father Gestalt therapy, believed that shame and embarrassment were "the quislings of the organism," the traitors that sold us out in adaptations to fears or other's demands.[6] His adversarial posture precluded understanding the gifts of the shame emotions in guiding us to growth and deeper spirituality, but he did use them as signposts to direct people to authentically be themselves rather than conform to stifling societal standards. "The summer of love" notwithstanding, most of middle class American culture in the sixties and early seventies was conformist, and many of the psychotherapies that emerged from that era were designed to "liberate" repressed emotion, thought, and impulse, and encourage authentic intimacy and expression. This particular workshop involves sixteen adults, most of whom have never met each other, sitting in a circle and watching the therapist, George, work with them one or two at a time. When it is sunny they sit outside, with spectacular views of the Pacific Ocean to the West and the pine covered mountains to the East. At night, or when it clouds up, they work in a cozy room in the lodge.

Perls pioneered the technique of the empty chair. He directed his clients to sit in front of an empty chair and speak to imagined others from dreams and from their past/present/future, with the goals of authentic current experience and transformative insight. He called the process "peeling the onion," because he experienced his clients (mostly products of the repressed forties, fifties, and early sixties) as having layers of adaptation concealing their true hearts.[7] In this he was anticipating the work of David Deida in supporting the liberation of deepest sexual essence, and Jeff Hawkins in explicitly examining internalized representations and consciously addressing them. We join the group on the second day. It's raining, and they are meeting in the lodge. Teresa volunteers to work and sits down in one of the two chairs in the center of the circle:

> Teresa: (Shaking slightly from feeling so exposed in front of the group, but yearning for some direction in dealing with her unfulfilling life.) "I want to work on my marriage."

George: (Taking a deep drag from his cigarette, he notices the tension in her jaw.) "Put your marriage in the chair and tell it how you feel."

Teresa: (Awkwardly she imagines her marriage with Preston in the chair opposite her. She immediately feels ashamed and reflexively avoids the emotion.) "I have a good marriage. My husband is successful, and my little boy is wonderful."

George: "I didn't ask for a character reference. Tell your marriage how you feel as you look at it."

Teresa: (*God, how can I feel so bad about my marriage?*) "I feel guilty."

George: "Guilt always hides resentment. Who do you resent?"

Teresa: (She responds without thinking.) "My husband, Preston."

George: "Put him in the chair and tell him what you resent."

Teresa: (Stuttering because her internal representation of herself is someone who never expresses her anger, she struggles to tell the truth.) "I … I resent you not listening to me, and staying out late."

George: (He sees where this is going and relaxes into his chair.) "Be your husband, and respond to Teresa." (He directs her to change places.)

Teresa: (As Preston she feels strangely strong and self-righteous.) "I make a good living and I love you and Aaron. A good wife appreciates her husband. Nobody's perfect, and men will be men. Just accept it and move on."

George: "Now be Teresa and respond."

Teresa: (She is shocked by her flood of rage as she sits down in the Teresa chair.) "A good husband doesn't cheat on his wife and lie like a coward about it." (Her voice is shaking with rage.)

George: "Is he hearing you?"

Teresa: "No, he just has that superior smirk."

George: "Show him how you feel."

Teresa: (To the surprise of the group and the delight of George, she stands up and kicks the Preston chair so hard it breaks.) "Fuck you! Fuck you for cheating and lying, and promising to be different, and then lying some more.

Fuck you, fuck you, FUCK YOU!" (She continues to kick the chair, crying and screaming.)

Later that evening, Teresa is by herself in the baths. Robin has hooked up with a psychologist from Fresno and is gone for the night, and Teresa is relaxing in the hot tub, staring out at the silver trail of the moon on the waters of the lagoon beneath the cliffs. Three men and two women from her group walk down the path and join her. After awhile, they are all talking about the workshop, and of course her work with George that afternoon quickly comes up. Edward, a chiropractor who drove down from Oregon for this workshop, asks her what she's going to do:

Teresa: "I don't know. Preston will never come to therapy with me. I don't know how I can make it as a single mother. I have no profession. We got married right out of college, and we wanted to start a family."

Edward: "I was afraid of being a single father, but it's been fine. I see my daughter half the week, and I'm on pretty good terms with my ex."

Teresa: (She's been married seven years and is not used to socializing with men without her husband nearby. She's enjoying the erotic polarity between her open feminine self and the trustable masculine presence of Edward, but doesn't quite consciously realize it at this moment. All she's aware of is curiosity about his life.) "You're divorced? What is it like? How do you do it?"

Edward: (He laughs and eases lower into the hot tub. Teresa likes his laugh.) "That's a lot of questions. Yeah, I'm divorced and I don't like it. I'm lonely. But I'd rather be lonely than married to the wrong woman."

Teresa: "How did you know she was the wrong woman?"

Edward: "Well, for one thing, she found out she was gay. There's not much I can do about being a guy."

Teresa: (She blushes with embarrassment, though nobody notices in the moonlight). "I'm so sorry. I didn't mean to pry. I mean …" (She literally doesn't know what to say.)

Edward: "That's OK. No need to apologize. She didn't know she was gay until we started practicing tantra together. The deeper we got into our sexuality the clearer it was to her that she was into women."

Teresa: (This is the kind of intimate conversation that she has only been able to have with her women friends. She leans forward, and Edward is very aware of the moonlight on her breasts.) "What's tantra?"

Four hours later, Teresa is covered in sweat, exhausted and breathless after her fifth orgasm. Edward is up on one elbow next to her, smiling, and looking into her eyes. She is wide open, and blocking nothing:

Teresa: "I've never enjoyed sex that much sober in my life. Or loaded either, now that I think of it. You're wonderful."

Edward: (He kisses her tenderly.) "You're wonderful." (David Deida maintains that the feminine grows best in the presence of loving praise, while the masculine grows best in the presence of loving challenge.[8] It's been years since Teresa has heard unqualified loving praise in bed with a man. It opens her to be more vulnerable and authentic.)

Teresa: "I don't know what I'll do when I get home."

Edward: "What do you want to do?"

Teresa: "Be with you." (They both laugh. Each knows that this is a workshop affair, and that she's not going to drop everything, divorce, and take her son to Oregon, even if Preston would OK his son moving to another state.) "I'm definitely divorcing Preston. I'd rather have no man than the wrong man."

Edward: "Then what?"

Teresa: "I enjoyed writing in college, and I loved my Philosophy of Law class. I think I'll be a legal secretary."

Edward: "Why not a lawyer?"

Teresa: "I don't think I could make it through law school. I was a good student, but you have to take the LSATs, apply, get in, and it's real competitive. I don't know if I'm smart enough." (She looks down.) "I feel so ashamed when I say that."

Edward: "Ashamed of what?"

Teresa: (She suddenly laughs, an open channel of emotion.) "Ashamed of thinking I might not be smart enough. Of course I am."

Edward: "I think you could do anything you want. If it feels right in your heart, go for it."

Teresa: "I'll never find another man like you."

Edward: "You could come visit, but I think it would be better to find a good man in Santa Barbara. You're a great woman. Long distance relationships suck, and you deserve love. Just find someone to work on it with you. That's what I'm going to do. In the beginning it's always magic, but you both need to work to keep love happening. I think Cindy and I could have made it if she hadn't been gay. Sometimes I wonder if I can find and keep a good woman." (He smiles sadly.) "A woman like you."

Teresa: (She hears his grief, and sees it in his face, which is open and unguarded. *"I can never really tell what Preston is feeling. He's always hiding. I'm not living like that any more."* She rubs her body against his and kisses his chest, offering erotic radiance and loving challenge.) "Just live up to who you are right now. I'm sure you'll be fine."

This is a third stage peak experience for Teresa and Edward. Both have been opened by the group with George, are further transported by the magic Esalen environment, and spend the evening serving each other. Edward, the masculine partner in their erotic polarity, anchors himself in deepest consciousness and leads the emotional/erotic dance into progressively deeper ecstasy. Teresa, the feminine partner, feels his trustable presence and his fully resolved commitment to know and claim her in the moment, and she responds with devotional love expressed through pleasure in her body. These are central masculine and feminine practices in third stage eroticism and life. Later as they talk, he offers her direction as to what he believes is best for her, unattached to whether she follows it or not. This direction resonates deeply in her heart and, several years later, she enrolls in law school and rediscovers John.

When Teresa feels ashamed in this dialog, she doesn't avoid it, but instead explores it with interest. Edward, in third stage harmony with her, supports this process without interrupting it. When he feels grief remembering his divorce, she offers him love through her body, the sweetest feminine gift. This level of relating looks and feels enormously simple when it happens, but is fiendishly hard to inhabit consistently. Most of us get a taste of it under the influence of romantic infatuation, which provides a biochemical vacation from our defenses. The added elements of third stage maturity in the above exchange were Edward and Teresa's utter candor, complete support of each other, and their willingness to examine emotional pain with interest and to embrace new behaviors and internal representations.

The tyranny of the bell curve.

All of us have both masculine and feminine aspects. Most happy couples trade places in their masculine/feminine polarity regularly, both sexually and otherwise. My wife is much more technically competent than I am, so she offers me direction on the computer, and I respond with appreciative surrender. Satisfied, uninhibited lovers will usually tell you that no matter how much they enjoy the masculine depth of consciousness/direction role, or the feminine devotional surrender through pleasure in the body role, they trade roles during lovemaking to some extent. Accomplished lovers feel these shifts and activate their masculine/feminine aspects accordingly to enhance polarity to open each other physically, emotionally, and spiritually. None of us fit exactly into the procrustean bed of *any* stereotype of how a man or woman should be, old or young, gay or straight.

Every culture has conformist standards that inform our internal representations of how we should be, and we'll often feel shame at discrepancies we perceive between ourselves and these representations. This shame is often projected as disapproval of others. I've seen it endlessly in my psychotherapy practice over the last thirty-four years. Gay "bears" (who find big, burly, hairy men the erotic ideal) being contemptuous of cross-dressing "fairies," being contemptuous of heterosexual transvestites. Unhappily married women being contemptuous of sexually active single women, being contemptuous of "promiscuous" men, being contemptuous of abstinent ascetics, being contemptuous of lusty, happily married housewives.

Shame *always* shows up in some fashion in our identities as masculine or feminine beings and, when it does, we can respond to it with first stage selfishness, second stage egalitarian tyranny of the "fair," or third stage surrender to opening ourselves and each other as far as we can.

The natural direction of development is toward integration into more complex, caring, and congruent internal representations of how we and others should be.[9] This means, *if unobstructed,* development naturally guides us to grow from first, to second, to third stage worldviews and practices. Clients often initially come into therapy telling me, "I don't think people can change." My response is often, "There is a core self-awareness that has the same flavor form birth to death, and all else is change. I believe therapy is about becoming more thoroughly your self. True discipline is using your will to do what the deepest, purest voice in you says serves the highest good, and not being distracted by lesser voices."

Significantly, becoming more thoroughly ourselves often involves embracing and integrating those aspects of us that vary from the norms of the cultures we're embedded in. If our culture says a strong man shouldn't enjoy feminine submissiveness, or that a good woman shouldn't get wildly lost in being ravished open erotically, men and women so wired will have barriers of shame to feel and resolve in embracing their deepest natures. Third stage masculine/feminine practices normalize embracing and integrating all experience, including the shame emotions, in the service of love.

1. Deida (1995, 1997, 2004)

2. Deida (2004)

3. Deida (2004)

4. Liedloff (1975)

5. Gottman (2001)

6. Nathanson (1987)

7. Perls (1968)

8. Deida (2004)

9. Wilber (2000)

6

Sexual Shame

From *The Ballad of Bill and Monica*

No,
He wouldn't want you,
touch you,
if he didn't care.
That's his problem,
nature,
is his flair.
Face it, you did it,
liked it,
liked him,
Just a little,
you loved him.

Maybe it's me, but I think
you'd try to entice him a little.
What a strange opportunity,
to have sex with,
sex with history.

There have been many examples of sexual shame in this book. Pam and Cecilia's shame at little Teresa and Sam's sexual play evoked the children's sexual shame at their mothers' horrified reactions. John's shame kissing Teresa on the beach by UCSB subtly intensified Teresa's shame at finding him sexually uninteresting. Teresa's hung over shame the morning after her seventeen-year-old drunken oral sex with Preston is another example.

Sexual shame can come from a variety of sources including things we choose or have chosen, things that were done to us without our choice, and discomfort that is conditioned into us by culture. We can choose to break sexual rules (as in Preston's infidelity), behave badly by our own sexual standards (as in Teresa's drunken oral sex), or discover ourselves the object of severe disapproval for some sexual feeling, thought, impulse, or behavior that initially felt innocent or harmless (as in the children's shame when they were discovered playing their looking/touching game). We can be ashamed at being victims of sexual deceit, sexual violence, or any disapproval. Different cultures with which we identify can indoctrinate us to feel shame for any number of sexual thoughts, feelings, behaviors or impulses and, no matter what our conscious control is over these activities, we will feel shame when we engage in them, and especially when we feel witnessed engaging in them. Let's briefly explore sexual shame from experiences we choose, experiences that involve little or no choice, and from cultural conditioning.

Shame from something sexual we choose.

We can choose to discuss sexual anatomy, physiology, or behavior, choose to make sexual overtures or respond positively or negatively to other's overtures, choose to masturbate, choose to display/hide our bodies, choose to purchase or pursue sexual imagery, garments, or paraphernalia, or choose to initiate or participate in any number of sexual practices. All of these constitute sexual choices that might elicit shame.

One of the best ways to understand sexual shame from something we have chosen is to imagine the memory, fantasy, or experience that has *most* turned us on and we *least* wish to reveal. OK, I've got mine, but I'm not going to tell it to you for the same reason you probably don't want to tell me yours. The fear of being found out, branded, and sentenced to shame and humiliation is similar to our fear of death; there is often a subjective sense that we risk annihilation if our secret is revealed. A great illustration of this process is the story of Ian and Shaun:

Ian and Shaun walk into a pub. They knock back a couple of pints, and Ian starts complaining. As he begins, the bartender smiles, rolls his eyes, and walks off to clean tables:

Ian: "Shaun, it's not right. I've roofed twenty-six cottages in our village, and do they call me 'Ian the roofer?'"

Shaun: (Sighing deeply.) "No, they don't."

Ian: "And Shaun, I've built beautiful benches and chairs, and anything you can imagine of wood, but do they call me 'Ian the wood-worker?'"

Shaun: (Looking out the window.) "No, they don't."

Ian: "But you fuck one goat...."

That's right, nobody wants to be publicly identified as Ian the goat-fucker, though many of us suffer secret shame at some forbidden aspect of our sexuality. Even the exceptions, the exhibitionists and serial killers who embrace public contempt, practice their forbidden activities in secret and hide meticulously for years, sometimes decades, before they are finally caught and trapped forever in the humiliation they unconsciously crave. Our *subjective experience* of the sexual part of us that we believe is most forbidden by the collective will usually be a source of sexual shame.

These forbidden choices can be represented on a continuum with non-exploitative sexual embarrassment on one end, and sexual exploitation of another person on the other. To put this in perspective, I've deliberately chosen goat-fucking as an extreme example of a sexually embarrassing choice, and serial killers as an extreme example of a sexually exploitative, violent, and evil choice (evil being defined as deliberately injuring another for personal gratification). I'm assuming that whatever your embarrassing memory, fantasy, or experience is, it will feel more acceptable (or *normal)* to you by comparison. Embarrassing masturbation fantasies would be towards poor Ian's end of the continuum, while coercing sex from an unwilling partner (for instance by whining, complaining, or negotiating) would be towards the serial killer end.

Normal

In general, what is *normal* to us depends on how wide an embrace we have of different perspectives. If consenting adults engaging in activities that are non-abusive and don't endanger their health is your standard for acceptable (read, "non-shameful") sexuality, then there is quite a wide range of activities you might be comfortable with. If you have elaborate rules (or internal representations; should-patterns) for acceptable sexual behavior (for instance, only with partners of the same religion, only between men and women, only when married, only in the dark, or only in certain positions), then there is a quite a wide range of what might be *subjectively erotic* thoughts or behaviors that will likely be shameful to you. For most of us, progressive development tends to involve an ever-widening range of what we feel is *normal* or *acceptable* sexuality. Whatever your standards for normal, your "most erotic/least wish to reveal" choice, like all shameful areas, can be a source of growth and transcendence.

Shame from something sexual where we have no choice.

Sexual shame also can come from things that we have little or no choice about. Victims of molestation and other forms of sexual violence are extreme examples. More common examples are shame coming from dreams, impulses, or fantasies that we discover more than create.

If left unprocessed and unexamined, we can emotionally injure or cripple ourselves for years or decades in response to events that we had no control over originally. An illustration of the power of unresolved victimization is reflected in the following excerpt from an individual therapy session that John had six years into his marriage with Teresa. Her son, Aaron, is fifteen and John's daughter, Ariel, is thirteen, and both children live half time with them in their Santa Barbara home. John began seeing Dr. Theo Brown (a local psychologist in private practice) because two of Teresa's friends said he was good with helping couples, especially with their sexual relationships. The following exchange occurs in their fourth session:

> Dr. Brown: "You said your sexual relationship with your first wife Annie was 'OK,' but I don't have a sense about how you two connected emotionally or erotically. That relationship has been somewhat invisible in our work so far." (He looks expectantly at John. Like most therapists, Theo knows that avoided material is usually fruitful ground, and often involves shame emotions.)

> John: (He shifts uncomfortably in his chair and looks away.) "We had problems, and there was something that happened."

> Dr. Brown: (He feels the intensity level rise in the room. *"Don't press too hard; there's a lot of emotional charge here."*) "Something happened?"

> John: "It's hard to talk about." (Theo waits patiently for ten seconds until John continues.) "Annie and I were at this party right after we got married, and I wanted to go and she wanted to stay. We had a little argument and, since we'd taken separate cars, I left. She wasn't drunk or anything; she didn't do that sort of stuff, but she had a few drinks and hung out with her friends for a couple more hours. When she was walking to her car, a man ..." (At this point John looks down and starts to cry.)

> Dr. Brown: (*"Very gently now."*) "A man ...?"

> John: (Suddenly it pours out.) "She was raped. A man dragged her into some trees and raped her at knife point, and I wasn't there to protect her. If only

I'd stayed, he wouldn't have attacked both of us. It was the worst thing that ever happened to her. She just couldn't get over it. Things were never the same with us after, even when Ariel was born." (He can't continue and keeps sobbing. Dr. Brown eases the story out. How the rapist was never caught, how the policemen looked at John as if he were responsible when he and Annie reported the rape that night, and how weak and impotent John has always felt about the whole trauma. Gradually John's distress eases, and they are talking with each other about the rape and its aftermath.)

Dr. Brown: "You seem ashamed of the event; even humiliated that you somehow didn't magically prevent it."

John: "Annie and her therapist told me lots of times that it wasn't my fault, but I can't help feeling somehow responsible that it happened."

Dr. Brown: "Your sense of a good man is someone who doesn't allow his wife to be raped after a party and, since it happened, you can't be a good man."

John: (He looks both surprised and relieved.) "Exactly."

Dr. Brown: "Would you feel that I wasn't a good man if the same thing happened to me and my wife?"

John: "No, not at all. I'd feel bad for you because I know how horrible it is for the husband as well as the victim, but I wouldn't blame you."

Dr. Brown: "First of all, you were a victim too. Annie experienced a catastrophic trauma, but everyone who loved her was also injured that night. That's how violence injures society, like the concentric ripples that spread out in a pool after a stone is thrown in. Secondly, we all have internal representations of how we should be that we refine throughout life. When we are self-aware enough we can use our conscious discernment to refine internal representations. Here, stand up and look into this mirror." (He urges John to his feet, and has him look into a sandstone-rimmed mirror hanging on the wall.) "See the man who tortures himself for not magically saving Annie from her rape. Look into his eyes with compassion and understanding." (As John does this, his body relaxes and his face becomes more mature and resolved.) "What's happening right now?"

John: "I don't know. I'm thinking about me, Annie, and the rape. Even though it was horrible and sad, I'm not as overwhelmed. I'm not ashamed."

Dr. Brown: "At this moment you have an internal representation that a good man can have bad things happen to those he loves and, even though he couldn't prevent them or fix them, he can still be a good man. I suggest that every time you feel ashamed about the rape, or of anything else, look into your eyes in a mirror until you shift into a more mature, compassionate perspective. Even if you do make a mistake, or hurt someone, endlessly suffering shame and humiliation solves nothing. There are better ways of making amends than self-flagellation."

John: (As he sits down and takes a sip of water, he has a sudden insight.) "Do you think this has anything to do with the sexual problems Teresa and I are having?"

Dr. Brown: (He smiles appreciatively. *"People become so wise when they can accept themselves and look for truth."*) "I suspect you're on to something."

Dr. Theo Brown knows that we have mirror neurons in our brain's orbitofrontal cortex (the area right behind our eyes) that reflexively reproduce other people's states of mind when we meet their gaze. This is the biological basis of empathy, and a major foundation for intimacy.[1] Remember John and Lon as toddlers looking into the loving eyes of their mothers and being quickly regulated from parasympathetic collapse back to happy sympathetic arousal. Theo has learned to utilize the multiple interlocking relationships of human consciousness to help his clients use this empathic capacity to self-regulate distress by looking into their own eyes in the mirror while cultivating compassionate understanding. He's found that this mobilizes states of consciousness that refine internal representations towards being more caring and realistic. States of consciousness have characteristic neural networks and firing patterns that strengthen every time they are evoked (a neuroscientist named Donald Hebb asserted in the 1950's that "Neurons that fire together wire together."[2]) The more we evoke a state of consciousness, the more likely that state is of becoming a stable trait. Psychotherapy mobilizes these capacities to help people tolerate and examine distress, refine internal representations, and adjust thoughts and behaviors towards health and growth.

In this session, John feels ashamed of Annie's rape, even though he had no control over it. Like all of us, he has reflexes to avoid productively examining his distress, thus compromising the self-reflective mechanisms necessary for acknowledging, allowing, and processing that are often necessary to refine internal representations. His avoidance locked him into a self-recriminating loop over Annie's victimization, and the resultant pain and inner conflict injured his first marriage and spilled over into interfering with healthy sexuality in his marriage with Teresa. With Theo's help, John feels his sexual shame, examines and refines his internal representations, and begins the process of opening himself to emotional, interpersonal, and sexual growth.

Culturally determined sexual shame and the incest taboo.

As we explored in Chapter One, shame at disapproval and pleasure at positive recognition are two of the major forces that shape human societies and maintain social systems. Since men are genetically programmed to be attracted to and penetrate the feminine, and women are programmed to offer erotic surrender to the claim of a powerful, present, high-status man, sexual shame is necessary to shape and maintain rules in every society. The classic example is the incest taboo which appears to be universal in human cultures. Anthropologists have yet to find any human group that routinely normalizes incest. Reasons for this are obvious. Cumulatively over thousands of years there are overwhelming adaptive advantages to not reproducing from within families of origin. The psychological and physical separation required to maintain the incest taboo is locked in sexual shame, and supported and maintained by culture. Some believe that the incest taboo is the basis of all repression and taboos.[3] I believe other forces also heavily influence sexual shame. Women are programmed to adorn themselves and offer feminine light to attractive males, and to have discriminative jealousy of other women who create intimate sexual polarities with their mates. Men are programmed to respond to the feminine shape with sexual pursuit, and to forbid other men sexual access to women they "possess." Position on personally important social hierarchies often involves, to varying degrees, our subjective and objective levels of sexual radiance and power.[4] Each of these genetically based drives involves approval/disapproval contingencies that potentially create elaborations of sexual shame that can cause unnecessary suffering (or be sources for awakening and expansion) at every level of development.

In most cultures, feminine people are shamed for displaying various aspects of their bodies and for engaging in various types of sexually explicit behavior, while masculine people are shamed for erotically claiming either the wrong feminine partner, or doing it in the wrong way.[5] Standards for skin display vary from culture to culture, but every culture has some version of shameful display. Standards for masculine claim vary from culture to culture, but every culture has some version of shameful erotic claim. One UCLA study from the eighties found that teen girls and boys had a mutually understood set of acceptable sexual behaviors *that had to happen in sequence* to be considered OK. For example, if a boy tried to touch a girl's breast before he kissed her, he was shamed. If he spent *even seconds* kissing first, the move to touch her breast was culturally acceptable whether she said "yes" or "no."

Unfortunately, in modern and postmodern society with our rampant unrealistic internal representations (expectation-patterns or should-patterns), sexual shame is generalized to an astonishing array of sexual and non-sexual behaviors. Teen girls are ashamed of being considered *too* sexual (as in, "She's a slut"), or *not sexual enough* (as in "She's so fat, she's just let her body go"). American women are supposed to look "good" (meaning sexually attractive), but not too provocative (as in, "I can't believe how short her skirt is"). Teen boys are encouraged to be sexually assertive with girls ("You should ask out that nice girl Sally"), but demeaned for their sexual yearning ("Guys only want one thing").

These messages are so destructive because they are *internalized.* In one study of rural culture in Indonesia, several villages were studied before and after the advent of TV. Before TV, there were no observable eating disorders among the teen girls. After a few years of TV, the village girls had the same rates of eating disorders (along with the corresponding distortions about body image and sexual attractiveness) as Western communities. Their culture changed in response to a new information source, and new sources of shame (for being too heavy, not sexy enough, or not fitting a TV inspired body-image ideal) were created. Internalized cultural sexual shame informs how we think, move, dress, touch, talk, play, and work. Try going to the movies with your zipper down or your blouse two extra buttons open, and you'll feel culturally determined sexual shame before the opening credits, *even if nobody besides you notices.*

Sexual shame can be a resource.

On a more positive note, forbidden material can enhance sexual arousal. Many culturally proscribed sexual fantasies and erotic games that individuals and couples find highly arousing have aspects that would be profoundly embarrassing if revealed to others (perhaps you discovered some of these in the exercise of imagining what most arouses you that you'd least like to reveal). Often these fantasies and games can provide enjoyable added charge to autoerotic and/or marital/relational sexual encounters. This erotic charge can be a goldmine for the individual and/or couple in creating and maintaining pleasure at every level from first to second to third stage lover relationships. Since development is include and transcend, we will never lose what we find erotic. Rather, if we face our desires and our shame courageously, we can discover and include what arouses us in a wider, deeper understanding and practice with ourselves and others. The original Kinsey studies in the late forties and early fifties showed American men peaking in sexual desire at nineteen and American women at thirty-nine.[6] I believe the explanation for this data is that nineteen-year-old men of that era were supported in being sexual beings, while young women were not. By thirty-nine, the women in the study had matured enough to expand their internal representations of a good woman to include an appreciation of the benefits of hot lovemaking, and had thus included and transcended their cultural conditioning of "good girls aren't sexually passionate or explicitly interested in great sex."

The answer to cultural confusion is *not* shaming either the process of breaking taboos or making taboos. As we become capable of self-reflection and response flexibility, we can feel, acknowledge, tolerate, and examine our shameful thoughts, impulses, and behaviors, and adjust them in ways that serve love and health. An example of this is the following excerpt from a therapy session with Dr. Theo Brown and John six weeks after John talked about Annie's rape:

John: "Teresa is still complaining that sex is boring. I have to agree. I enjoy it, but it's not the most exciting thing in the world. Maybe that only happens in movies."

Dr. Brown: "I've suggested that you and Teresa come in as a couple to work on this, and you keep refusing. What's that about?"

John: "I don't know. Sex is so private."

Dr. Brown: "Are there things that you haven't told Teresa about your sexuality?"

John: (He looks down and blushes, and then visibly cycles through humiliation and rage.) "What is it with you? Is that all you're interested in, my sexual fantasies? What fucking business is it of yours? Do you get off on them or what?"

Dr. Brown: (*"Make it safe for him to explore. He's almost ready to deal with whatever it is."* Looking calmly into John's eyes, he speaks gently.) "This feels like an exposed nerve of some sort."

John: (Now he's embarrassed by his outburst.) "I'm sorry. I shouldn't have gone off like that."

Dr. Brown: "That's nice of you but," (he laughs a little,) "I'm actually glad you trust me enough to get pissed off at me. It makes me curious. You report not having much erotic energy with Teresa, but there was a lot of energy just now. It sounds like you have some sexual fantasies that disturb you."

John: "What can I do? Do we really *choose* what turns us on? I can't help it if I'm warped."

Dr. Brown: (*"Finally. I think he and I are solid enough to deal with the material, whatever it is."*) "OK, now I'm *really* curious. If you trust me enough, tell me what you're talking about."

John: "Well, I have fantasies about raping Teresa. That's so sick, especially after what happened to Annie."

Dr. Brown: "I really don't know what you mean my 'raping' her. Maybe you could walk me through the fantasy. I assume it's a masturbation fantasy, and all of us have been conditioned to be ashamed of masturbation to start with. Just describe the details."

John: (Reluctant, but seeing approval and affection in Theo's eyes, he dives in.) "Well, she's naked and walking around the house, and I'm somewhere watching her. Then I break in, grab her, throw her down on the bed, and fuck her really hard."

Dr. Brown: (*"Most of these are so tame. Don't get distracted. Stay focused on helping him."*) "In the fantasy, what kind of an experience is she having?"

John: "She's a little scared a first, but then, no," (His eyes widen a little in sudden understanding,) "She's having lots of orgasms and is really into it."

Dr. Brown: "That's ravishment. David Deida says that violently taking a woman with love is ravishment, while violently taking a woman with anger, fear, and shame is rape.[7] Most women *love* being ravished at least once in awhile. Check out a few romance novels if you don't believe me. Sixty percent of the books sold in America are romance novels bought by women, and the heroines are ravished all the time."

John: "But isn't that disrespectful? Shouldn't you ask a woman if she's ready?"

Dr. Brown: "Talk to Teresa about this. Most women like their man to know when they are interested and to make overtures that they find enjoyable. 'Would you like to have sex right now?' is low on the list of favorite overtures for most of the women I've known."

John: "But isn't it sick to have rape fantasies?"

Dr. Brown: "First of all, a fantasy is not an act. You can have whatever fantasy you want, and nobody is injured. Since men are programmed to want variety in their sexual partners, thank God we have fantasies to provide that in monogamous relationships. Our hunter-gatherer ancestors were programmed not only to bond romantically with one woman and to care for and protect their families, but also to pursue and ravish feminine erotic radiance when they saw it. Men that didn't pursue the feminine couldn't compete genetically with men that did. In our monogamous, egalitarian society, it doesn't work for men to pursue lots of women. Most women won't stand for it, and mature intimacy that can improve over decades seems to require monogamy."

John: "I don't know how to talk about this with Teresa."

Dr. Brown: "Of course not. Western society is miserable at teaching kids, teens, and adults how to feel, accept, and talk about explicit sexual material. I think you two are ready to come in as a couple."

John: "OK, I finally get it. Teresa said she'd come in any time. Let's set up a session."

Theo isn't focusing particularly on *why* John has ravishment fantasies. He's focusing on the core energetic exchange of the fantasy. It is useful in making sense of our life story to understand aspects of why we are the way we are, but that doesn't change our basic orientations. In my experience as an individual therapist, marriage counselor, and sex-therapist, the include-and-transcend rhythm of sexual development means that you don't undo sexual programming. Changing current programming usually involves including it in a larger, wider embrace. As we grow, we discover what turns us on. To some this is like discovering jewels, while to others it's like discovering monsters. Either way, erotic charge needs to be honored, and any charge, when infused with love, can be beautiful and ultimately integrated into growth.[8] To do this usually requires the courage to feel and tolerate our shame, self-reflect on our internal representations and on the nature of our eroticism, and find ways to accept and develop. If someone does have an erotic charge around destructive activity, the *energetic exchange* of the arousing fantasy needs to be honored to support integration into a larger, more loving, positively transformative system. For instance, if John found it sexually arousing to actually see terror on his partner's face, he might find the interface of dark power and utter vulnerability erotically charged, and could thus integrate that interface with love into his erotic imagery and practice.

The collective can be threatened by differences.

Every culture has sexual taboos, and thus institutionalized sexual shame. Consciousness allows us to continue to differentiate and integrate throughout life on most developmental lines, including the interpersonal, psychosexual, moral, and cognitive lines. The human advantage is that we can direct our own individual evolution all the way to oneness with everything where there is no shame because there is no other.[9] The individual disadvantage is that the more we differentiate from the values of the cultures we're embedded in, the more skillful means we need to use to not be perceived as threats to the collective and thus evoke attack from the collective. A pride of lions will kill a female from another pride. She is different and therefore a threat that warrants violence. Similarly, if we appear to have moral standards, or should-patterns, that are visibly different from the cultures we're embedded in, those cultures will often instinctively attack either actively (think Jesus on the cross) or passively (as in religious orders shunning moral offenders).

Carl Jung called growing different from the collective as becoming "inflated" beyond the collective's comfort zone (the cultural window of tolerance for differences). An inflated individual cues the collective to either destroy the offender or pull him or her back down into the commons. The collective sometimes can't distinguish between perspectives that are genuinely harmful (like criminals lying, cheating, stealing, or engaging in other violence for egocentric gains), and perspectives that are genuinely superior ("turn the other cheek," and "do unto others as you would have others do unto you" were originally threatening to Roman culture). Since we often have difficulty consciously examining differences in should-patterns because of the shame they can evoke, even potentially superior perspectives are often attacked before they are evaluated.

Most conformist perspectives avoid facts if they conflict with biases, and most worldviews resist pressure to change. This results in one of the burdens of conscious development; the principle of "greater depth, less span."[10] The deeper we go on any developmental line, the fewer will join us there and, since we are social creatures, the lonelier we risk becoming. The need for intimates of comparable depth on different developmental lines is certainly one of the reasons that Buddhism includes sangha (association with like minded peers) as one of the three jewels of its traditions, along with dharma (teachings), and Buddha (the exemplar of liberation).

The take home message here is that we all bear the burden of sexual shame and that, if examined, processed, and integrated, this shame can be a wellspring of intimacy, pleasure, growth, and development.

1. Siegal (2005), Gibson (2006)

2. Hebb (1949), Siegal (1999)

3. Barratt (2005)

4. Buss (1999)

5. Gilbert (2002)

6. Kinsey (1948), (1953)

7. Deida (1997)

8. Deida (2006)

9. Wilber (1995)

10. *Ibid*

7

The Wisdom of Laughter

From *Difficult*

I didn't crash my best friend's car
Didn't get busted at Murphy's Bar
Didn't get pregnant at 17
Or blow the trust fund on coke and weed
Wasn't me who left the iron on
And burned up the basement at grandpa's farm
You maxed my card on your trip to Rome
And had to call up Daddy for another loan

So no, don't you call me difficult
You have no idea how hard it really is

"Humor starts with a man in trouble."
Jerry Lewis[1]

Here are John and Teresa at home discussing his session. It's six PM and they're sitting on their front porch, having a glass of wine. John, who is a Superior Court Judge, recessed early when the defense rested on an assault case, and Teresa, a lawyer for legal aid, successfully blocked the eviction of one of her clients from their low cost housing, and is basking in the glow of a battle won:

Teresa: "Theo's right about 'Do you want to have sex right now?' being a turn off. It's like, 'Do you want to do the dishes?' or, 'Do you want to wash the car?' or …"

John: (Embarrassed but laughing.) "OK, I get it. It's a turn off. Why didn't you ever tell me?"

Teresa: "I don't know. I was afraid your feelings would get hurt, and I've never thought about it when we weren't about to do it."

John: "How would you like me to ask?"

Teresa: (She looks out at the Channel Islands, and takes a sip of wine. The evening is peaceful and they can see the sun setting through the clouds on the Pacific horizon.) "I'd like you to pick a good time and just do it; just take me. I don't want to have to decide or think about it." (She looks down.)

John: "You're blushing."

Teresa: (Now she laughs.) "It's embarrassing. I'm a career woman, a respected attorney, who has to walk into court and kick ass, and what I want is to be swept away."

John: (Smiling, he puts his arm around her and feels protective and attracted.) "You mean, ravished?"

Teresa: "Yes Tarzan. Me Jane, take me." (They both laugh as the wine and intimate talk are conspiring to loosen them up and turn them on.)

John: "You've got it, baby." (He kisses her passionately, and she relaxes into his arms. John leads her inside and they have their best sex in months.)

There was a lot of laughter in this conversation. Embarrassment and laughter often go hand in hand.[2] Right at the interface of forbidden feelings, impulses, thoughts, and behaviors there is emotional charge that can turn into spontaneous responses like laughing, crying, or screaming, sometimes in combination.[3] Go to the Zoo and check out a troop of monkeys, and you'll see extreme versions of emotional responses expressed through their bodies as they groom, fight, trick, caress, have sex, and flee. In humans these physiological capacities appear early in development and become intimately intertwined with consciousness. An infant smiles at five weeks, can laugh when tickled at ten weeks, and can fully release into both laughter and raging tantrum at sixteen to twenty-one weeks.[4]

Laughter, like shame, continues to be elaborated into a variety of individual and social experiences. Some laughter is release of tension at discovering that a perceived threat is not a threat at all. Physical humor is driven by initial distress at empathetic connection to a pratfall, and then relief when we realize it is not us who has fallen. Much conversational laughter is not connected with anything observably funny, but instead seems to be a sort of social lubricant.[5] Jokes usually involve setting up a universe with one set of rules, and then delivering a punch line that surprisingly shifts perspectives to make us laugh.[6] This is consistent with Sylvan Tomkins' hypothesis that sudden shifts in emotional intensity evoke laughter.[7]

The neural pathways for pain, fear, and laughter are intimately connected.[8] The terror of a roller coaster is expressed through our bodies in delighted screams, while pain and panic can cause us to scream in horror or despair. Crying can arise with overwhelming loss, pain, fear, sadness, joy, or love, and can help us integrate such experiences, refining our internal representations. With loss, crying is a major resource for healing. We can also laugh until we cry, but without the release of cortisol, prolactin, and magnesium that characterize tears of sadness and other strong emotions.[9] Laughter often arises when we encounter shameful or embarrassing areas, and helps us deal with the forbidden, the unspoken, and the perspectives that we resist, even as they fascinate us.[10] These capacities are necessary for physical and emotional health. For example, men who are able to cry are less prone to stomach ulcers,[11] while laughing watching a funny film is physiologically like a jolt of aerobic exercise.[12]

Much of humor deals with shame and surprise.[13] We learn to avoid shameful experiences but a comedian can guide us into embarrassing territory and surprise us with a new perspective (a punch line or a gag) that results in pleasurable laughter. Since we are all programmed to avoid shame to varying degrees, the capacity to *enjoyably* encounter a shameful area creates the possibility for new perspectives and new integration. Integrating shameful areas into a more coherent sense of self can make us smarter, deeper, more flexible, and better connected socially.

Later that night, John and Teresa are watching TV while their cat, Carl, is stalking a bird that is perched on the other side of the screen of an open window. Suddenly the bird sees Carl and launches out into the yard, just as Carl pounces and hits the screen, first clawing it and then falling backwards onto the sofa. Both John and Teresa start laughing while embarrassed Carl scoots out of the room:

> Teresa: (Concerned about Carl's hurt feelings, she gets up to follow him. John is laughing so hard he can't move.) "We're sorry, Carl. We didn't mean to laugh at you for falling."
>
> John: "Speak for yourself. Boy, this is turning into a great night." (This cracks him up even more.)
>
> Teresa: (Smiling, but reproving.) "That's mean. How would you feel if people were laughing so hard at you?"

John: "If I tried to jump through a screen to eat a bird, I'd deserve it." (This gets them both going again, though Teresa has made a good point. Many consider laughter a function of hostility, dominance display, or indirect expressions of hostile or libidinous drives.[14])

Men tend to laugh at physical humor and jokes (more hostility and dominance driven), while women tend to be more moved to laughter by funny contexts and stories (more social connection driven.[15]) A group of women eating lunch will laugh easily about different aspects of their experience, while a group of men will more likely laugh at jokes or put-downs. Men and women share the capacity to direct anger and project shame onto others. Such contempt and humiliation is the foundation of much humor. The popularity of Howard Stern, Rush Limbaugh, Don Rickles and many comics lies in their ability to demean and humiliate others publicly. Interesting, many comedians, especially women, evoke laughter by demeaning themselves. In the above example, John evoked Teresa's laughter by offering the humiliating image of himself jumping through a screen to eat a bird.

Contempt and humiliation.

Anger and disapproval directed outward is often experienced as contempt. Humiliating another is attacking them with the intent to demean. Being humiliated involves *feeling* publicly demeaned; a subjective experience that might not involve another actual person since we can react to imagined experiences in our past/present/future.[16]

From an evolutionary psychology perspective, both contempt and humiliation are aspects of the shame emotions that can protect a tribe from loss. Anger expressed symbolically doesn't kill. Humiliation *offered* satisfies urges to do violence. Humiliation *endured* can become an initiatory ordeal that potentially cleanses a tribal member and allows everyone to experience a redemption or rebirth. This process can be observed in the ritual humiliations and submissions that are involved in many rites of initiation.

What makes us laugh at demeaning ourselves, our friends, or our enemies? What is so funny about a celebrity roast (making fun of a popular figure) or telling a thoroughly embarrassing personal story? Something surprising and embarrassing about another or ourselves involves sudden shifts in emotional intensity, a hallmark of humor.[17] The shock of physical humor and the double meanings inherent in much spoken humor often involve surprising swoops of emotion.[18] Contempt and humiliation involve not just new perspectives and shifts in emotional intensity, but actual attacks on others or ourselves; attacks that, *if they evoke laughter*, are socially permissible and can actually enhance social status.

Humiliation humor is a way of experiencing and examining taboo behavior without the requirements of physical punishment and retribution. *The Aristocrats* is a documentary film that involves dozens of comedians telling the same joke about abuse and incest in surprising ways, breaking endless language, image, and sexual taboos until the punchline ("What's the name of your act?" answered by, "The Aristocrats") that attacks the privileged upper classes. Attacking high status individuals violates taboos, thus often evoking surprise and suddenly shifting levels of emotional intensity, while adding the forbidden pleasure of acting *as if* we were higher on the social hierarchy than our target. Demeaning our enemies adds the satisfaction of indulging our desires to strike out, but without having to actually kill, injure, or risk injury. Physical assault is dangerous physically, psychologically, and socially for everyone concerned, and is potentially irreversible (as with killing or crippling). Humiliating another is a form of psychological assault that, if skillfully done in ways that elicit laughter, can *deescalate* dangerous situations while satisfying emotional hunger for violence.

Our hunter-gatherer forebears' capacities to "make fun of" others gave evolutionary advantages to tribes where high status members or enemies could be attacked with relative impunity using humor, thus providing stress release and social positioning in the instinctual struggle to inhabit position on personally important social hierarchies. Such tribes were also less likely to have valuable members killed or driven out when they evoked rage in powerful others (especially rage from alpha males). The offender could be humiliated, made an object of ridicule, and be laughed at, often with the option of enduring with fortitude. Enduring other's humiliating laughter actually can have a redemptive benefit for the individual and the group as demonstrated by the initiate enduring humiliation rather than physical danger in many rites of passage. There is also the option of *joining* others in laughing at ourselves, thus demonstrating shared perspectives and shared membership. In all these displays of violence through humor, a tribe has enormously reduced risk of losing members to physical violence while balancing psychic energies and establishing a more stable social hierarchy. During the dark ages, the Jester had a homeostatic effect at court. He could say forbidden things as jest, and so reduce tensions while avoiding personal retribution.[19] Effective humor is thus a physically non-violent way to establish and maintain position on social hierarchies and to balance forbidden social energies that can't be safely addressed more directly.

Erotic humiliation

We often laugh at the erotic humiliation of others. In the movie, *American Pie,* the signature comic scene was a protagonist suddenly discovered having intercourse with an apple pie. This is classic erotic humiliation, being discovered or observed breaking a sexual taboo, or coerced by another into breaking a sexual taboo. Most of us find some depictions of erotic humiliation funny, whether they are personally sexy or not. "His lover makes him eat dog food out of a dish on the floor," was a punch line used in a *Hill Street Blues* episode in the 80's that did nothing for me sexually, but seemed hilarious when delivered by the victim's ex-wife at a formal dinner party.

Laughter, humiliation, and eroticism all involve charged emotions that can be experienced alone or in combination. Often where there is public laughter there is secret erotic charge. We tend to be aroused (though often ashamed) by our own most charged fantasy of surrendering to or offering erotic humiliation, and can find it preferable to laugh rather than acknowledge such arousal. It was easy to laugh at Monica and Bill in the Oval Office, but potentially harder to acknowledge the eroticism of a woman on her knees having slavish oral sex with a dominant partner. Most of us secretly have a version of erotic humiliation that is profoundly arousing. Ask yourself, "What form of humiliation or surrender to humiliation do I find erotically charged in fantasy or reality?" I could offer personal examples but, probably like you, I wouldn't want to reveal my own subjectively forbidden impulses. Suffice to say, out of a hundred erotic humiliation scenarios, most of us would find some disgusting, some turn-ons, some funny, and/or some neutral. Most of these activities presented in surprising ways with sudden shifts of emotional intensity, *in ways that were not too humiliating for us personally,* would likely evoke laughter.

Laughter, shame, and integration

Psychotherapy is very much about finding the habitual barriers to perceiving immature or distorted internal representations and helping clients to tolerate the painful emotions, discern the internal representations, and refine behaviors and representations towards health, growth, and happiness. Most therapists will tell you that when you can get a client laughing about their neurotic behavior, you have made significant progress. I encourage my clients to be entertained by their distortions and defenses, and to laugh at their defensive patterns and behaviors. "What's the big deal?" I'll ask, "We're all going to die, the earth will eventually be consumed by our exploding star, and our petty humiliations and defenses are less than insignificant specks of dust in the universe. Let's enjoy them while we can."

1. Carr (2006)

2. Dobson (2006)

3. Carr (2006)

4. *Ibid*

5. *Ibid*

6. *Ibid*

7. Nathanson (1987)

8. Carr (2006)

9. Crepeau (1992)

10. Carr (2006)

11. Parachin (1992)

12. Bjerklie (2006)

13. Nathanson (1987)

14. Carr (2006)

15. Shulman (2006)

16. Gilbert (2002)

17. Nathanson (1987)

18. Shulman (2006)

19. Carr (2006)

8

Shame and Our Personal Myth

From, *Comfort*

Some give with love from skies above
each one does his part.
Some give from noble purpose
straight through the heart.

I know that most people try
to give what they can,
if it's just to offer up
one focused glance.

Yes ... it's alright
Oh ... we'll be fine
Yes ... it's alright

We are all the central figures in our own personal myth. Each one of us exists at the center of a unique universe we are born into and die from. Some healing systems such as narrative therapy deal almost exclusively with helping individuals identify, explore, and refine their personal life story (also known as autobiographical narrative, life myth, and individual archetype). Interpersonal neurobiologists have established that one of the strongest predictors of good relationships, healthy functioning, and liberation from temperamental and personality limitations is a positive life story that makes sense to the individual.[1] This is what attachment researchers call a "coherent autobiographical narrative."[2] Carl Jung referred to the process of creating a positive life myth as individuation;[3] constructing a life story that makes sense of the past, present, and future, and that involves feeling like the active architect of a worthwhile life where we are connected with all beings. The relative ability to identify, feel, tolerate, and effectively process shame is a central determinant of progress in these activities, and a central block if it is ignored or mishandled.

There are endless perspectives that can be utilized in exploring life stories including egocentric ("Am I getting my needs met?"), conformist ("Am I living my life according the ancient wisdom of my sacred Book?"), and rational ("Am I maximizing my profit and position on personally important hierarchies?"). This chapter will explore autobiographical narrative with John and Teresa's family from a mythological/symbolic perspective, an interpersonal neurobiological perspective, and an Integrally informed perspective. I've chosen these three since mythological/symbolic is largely subjective, interpersonal neurobiological is largely scientific/objective, and Integrally informed finds value in all perspectives.

Like the canary in the mineshaft, conflict is often the first sign in a story that something needs attention.

Teresa is having a dream she's had before. She and John are walking down a city street at night and there is a vague sense of menace in the air. Shockingly, two men step out of nowhere and demand their wallets. John weakly protests and one man smacks him across the head, sending him tumbling to the ground. Teresa tries to scream as she bends down to tend to him, but is grabbed from behind. She wakes terrified and sits up abruptly, waking John.

Teresa: "Not another one."

John: "Another nightmare?" (She nods and he rolls over to comfort her, but she shrugs him off.) "What?"

Teresa: "It was two men attacking us. They knocked you down and reached for me."

John: "And you're pissed *at me* for that?"

Teresa: "I'm sorry. I know it doesn't make any sense. It's the same kind of thing each time. We're together, you get hurt, and I'm powerless."

John: "I can't help your dreams. Besides, I'd protect you if we got attacked." (Teresa looks at him skeptically, and this *really* makes him mad.) "OK. I am too mad to talk. We can deal with this in therapy tomorrow." (They both go back to sleep, isolated from each other and unhappy.)

The next day they're in Dr. Theo Brown's office describing the episode:

Dr. Brown: "What do you think these dreams are telling you Teresa?

Teresa: (Squirming a little and looking away from John, she speaks slowly.) "I hate to say it, but I guess I don't trust John to stand up for me."

John: "You have no reason to believe that. I don't get it."

Dr. Brown: "Just think for a moment about what your life story is."

Teresa: "What do you mean?"

Dr Brown: "Before we're born we begin learning through our senses without conscious awareness or focal attention. At eighteen months we can have explicit conscious memories that require focal attention. By three years we have a sense of past, present, and future, and at five years our brain is mature enough to have a sense of our autobiography, or life story. Soon after that we can see ourselves as central figures in the history of our lives, and that's auto-biographical narrative or our personal life myth. We tend to organize an amazing amount of meaning from how we interpret and inhabit our personal myths; our autobiographical narratives."

Teresa: "Well, my story is things are tough and I ultimately have to take care of me and my son by myself. Men are nice, but they will always let me down."

John: "My story is that I'll always do my best to do right and never get credit for being good. People will always misjudge and disrespect me. I'll be faithful, but the asshole will get the girl. I'll do the work, but the guy who kisses the boss's ass will get the credit."

Dr. Brown: "Wow. These are pretty bleak stories. What would you like them to be?"

Teresa: "I want to know my man will die for me. I want to believe that I deserve to be able to do the work I can do well, and then come home to a house full of love."

John: "I'd die for you."

Teresa: "I can feel the truth of it." (She tears up.) "But something is missing. I don't know if it's me, or you, or what."

Dr. Brown: "The number one predictor of secure attachment with a spouse or a child is for someone to have a coherent autobiographical narrative where their life makes sense *to them*. I think you two need some work having your lives make sense."

John: "What difference does it make? The facts are the facts. Our life story is our life story. We should lie to ourselves to feel better? That feels phony."

Dr. Brown: "What you believe now is phony. A true warrior is someone who does what's right even thought he's scared. That's you, John. Look at all you've had to go through to be a judge and be with Teresa. Look at how honorable you've been with her and the kids and how much integrity you have on the bench. Look at how you've learned to confront your family's expectations to accommodate them. What's false is your refusal to feel the power and joy of your warrior nature and to channel that joyful power into knowing and claiming Teresa."

John: "But she thinks I'm a wimp in her dreams."

Dr. Brown: (He feels attuned to John and comfortable offering him masculine challenge. *"How do I wake him up?"*) "That's her problem. Your job is to feel your integrity, power, humor, and shadow, and claim her from those things every day. As you do this you gradually mature to understand and inhabit your life as a more beautiful, good, and true autobiographical narrative. Try this story, 'As a child I learned how to be strong and feel weak. As I matured I learned how to honor my strength and integrity.'"

Teresa: "I like that. It's true John. That's you." (He glows in response. One of the sweetest things in the world to a masculine person is feminine devotional love.) "But what about my story?"

Dr. Brown: "When you chose John, what were you hoping for?"

Teresa: (She looks down.) "I thought I could feel loved and safe at the same time."

Dr. Brown: "How do you stop yourself from doing that?"

Teresa: "It's hard to trust. It's hard to surrender."

Dr. Brown: "Can you feel into John's heart and know when he deserves your trust and surrender?"

Teresa: "If I concentrate on it I can."

Dr. Brown: "Does he deserve it right now?" (She looks searchingly into his eyes. John looks back relaxed and present.)

Teresa: "Yes he does." (As she speaks, her face and body become visibly more radiant and desirable. John unconsciously leans toward her, drawn by her light.)

Dr. Brown: "All right." This is more like it."

John: (Suddenly he looks away.) "Why do I feel self-conscious all of a sudden?"

Dr. Brown: "Self conscious? Could you describe more of what you're feeling in your body?"

John: "Embarrassed. Ashamed. God knows why. Damn! Why does this happen?" (Teresa slumps, and her light dims.)

Dr. Brown: "This is good. What's the internal representation below the shame? What is the should-system that you just violated? Be interested John."

John: (Speaking slowly, clearly turning deeply inward, he explores his shame.) "I'm not supposed to feel strong and brave. I shouldn't feel too good about myself or …"

Dr. Brown: "Or …?"

John: "I don't know. All I can think of is when my family was in therapy and it was all about my father cheating, or my mother feeling ripped off, or my brother getting into trouble."

Dr. Brown: "It was never about you being strong and brave?" (John and Teresa both start laughing.) "What's makes you guys laugh?"

Teresa: "John is so much the normal one in that family. You'd have to go to a Thanksgiving or a wedding to see it. He's just this normal person and they're so intense."

John: "I can just hear my brother making sarcastic comments about me being strong and brave."

Dr. Brown: (He gestures to an empty chair.) "Imagine him here. Speak to him. Respond to his sarcasm."

John: (Surprising Teresa, his voice intensifies with anger.) "Back off, Al. Being a loser is not that cool. My life is good. My woman is great. And I'd walk through fire for her or for my principles. Can you say that? I don't think so."

Teresa: "That would shut him up."

Dr. Brown: "What's the expression on his face?"

John: "He's ashamed and so am I." (He turns back to his imagined brother.) "I'm sorry, Al. I don't want you to feel bad. I just want you to be happy and back off."

Dr. Brown: "So what's the internal representation behind your shame? Feel the shame and the sense of transgression. What rule are you breaking?"

John: "I'm not supposed to publicly talk about my successes or Al's failures. It's just not right. That sounds so messed up."

Dr. Brown: "What is a more compassionate and mature standard for dealing with your successes and other's failures?"

John: (Relaxing as he reaches for more care and depth of understanding.) "I should enjoy everyone's successes including mine. I should have compassion for everyone's failures including mine." (He catches Teresa smiling radiantly at him.) "What's up with you?"

Teresa: "This feels like showing up. I can't imagine the man you are now being the guy in my dreams."

Dr. Brown: "So, Teresa, what might your new story be?"

Teresa: "I have a warrior for a husband and I deserve it." (Now John glows. This is a standard that he can wholeheartedly commit to.)

The Warrior archetype tends to be especially important to masculine people as does the Goddess archetype of being a wide open channel of love and emotion to feminine people. Myamoto Mushashi, the preeminent sword fencer of seventeenth century Japan, wrote *A Book of Five Rings* about the Way of the Warrior.[4] In it he asserted that resolute acceptance of death, rigorous honesty, self-discipline, expanding depth of consciousness, and constant commitment to deepest life's purpose were organizing principles in the Way of the Warrior. Three hundred and fifty years later, his words ring true to masculine people. This is a powerful and universal archetype, but it is only one of many. Each personal myth has it's own unique healthy and unhealthy aspects and can guide us towards either transcendence or self-destruction.

Our personal myth: adolescent self-destruction or mature transcendence?

Humans have always understood that each life is a drama with intense themes and absorbing characters. This seminal understanding is reflected in the myths and legends that permeate every human culture. From the ancient story of Gilgamesh who dedicated his life to trying to undo the death of his best friend[5], to the *Godfather* movies of Frances Ford Coppola chronicling how power corrupts even when used in service of family and love, humans have created stories that speak to us in universal themes that we can apply to ourselves. Carl Jung[6] and Joseph Campbell[7] popularized integrating these primal human stories into the development of individuals. They rightly observed that cultural myths are most useful when they inspire us to discover and fully take responsibility for our own unique personal dramas. These dramas tend to fall into two general categories, adolescent self-destruction and mature transcendence.

Myths of adolescent self-destruction.

Achilles chose a short glorious life over a long happy one.[8] This is similar to a study done on Olympic athletes in which a phenomenal number said they would happily shave decades off their lives if only they could win Olympic Gold. Aphrodite essentially condemned two cultures (Troy and Greece) because her vanity was wounded by Helen being judged *by one guy* as more beautiful that her. Jehovah, in response to being teased and challenged by Lucifer, killed all of Job's family, destroyed his farm, and covered him with sores. These stories reflect the mythological orientation of five to eleven year olds who believe superpowers can and should control the world with various forms of egocentric indulgence or primitive black and white, eye for an eye, moral reasoning. Most of us develop internal representations informed by myths of this type, and we can be ashamed when we don't live up to their unrealistic or selfish demands. If we can identify, feel, and tolerate this shame, and readjust our internal representations to be more caring, we can use these internal stories as jumping off places for mature development. If not, we are destined to keep repeating the same tired dramas. This dichotomy is reflected in the following excerpt from an individual session that John had with Dr. Brown the week after he and Teresa processed her dream:

John: "I've been thinking a lot about the Warrior."

Dr. Brown: "Yes."

John: "I don't think I get it. Am I supposed to be like the Terminator? You know, kick ass all the time like Jet Li?"

Dr. Brown: (Laughing.) "God, I hope not. What do you think?"

John: "It seems more subtle than that. But standing up to Al in the last session felt so good, and acknowledging my own power seems so right. Now I think I'd be ashamed to back down from anybody."

Dr. Brown: "So, to you at this point, a warrior has to kick ass if threatened. He loses his choice to do anything else. If he does back down he should feel ashamed." (John nods his head.) "That's certainly consistent with every comic book, adventure story, and many myths, but is it the deepest truth to you?"

John: (Suddenly he is completely the mature Superior Court Judge.) "Of course not. Violence of any sort should always be the last resort."

Dr. Brown: "You don't seem to feel ashamed at this moment."

John: "No, I can see what's right. It's just when these sticky embarrassing personal situations happen that I get confused."

Dr. Brown: "A Shaman friend of mine named Jade Wahoo once told me that men gradually inhabit the Warrior during the first part of their lives. They take risks, they make mistakes, and they learn when and how to best stand firm or gracefully yield. Gradually they create a life story with personal meaning, grow with new experience and insight, and then, usually in their fifties, are initiated into the archetype of Man of Wisdom where serving the highest good becomes a major organizing principle of their life.[9] Along the way they learn to feel their shame and reach beneath it for mature wisdom rather than impulsively act from it to try to prove something to themselves or others."

John: "I'm attracted to that. But it's hard with Teresa."

Dr. Brown: "What's hard?"

John: "She gets so disgusted when I'm weak."

Dr. Brown: "How often is she right? How often are you not being your best self and then collapsing into shame or anger when you're challenged, instead of going deeper and growing?"

John: "Less now than before. She's right a lot, but she's so insulting some-times when she's mad that it's hard to keep a hold of myself and love her through the humiliation. She's usually great when I can do it."

Dr. Brown: "It's beautiful that you know your mission is to hold onto your-self and love her when she reflects your shadow (the parts of you that are hard to see). You've grasped a central aspect of the warrior archetype. This is Jet Li risking his life for the highest good, not just for egoic gratification."

Myths of mature transcendence.

In the Tolkien Trilogy, *The Lord of the Rings,* there is a curious morality play repeated throughout the books. One by one, the major characters are tempted by the Ring of Power.

Tom Bombadil (the nature mystic) is too committed to his forest and his wife Goldenberry to have any interest in power over others. He is the ultimate tribal member, disconnected from the larger sentient world. He tosses the ring into the air, makes it vanish and, to Frodo's amazement, puts it on and doesn't disappear. He has no interest in extending his power in any way. The dark side of this is his total lack of interest in using his considerable gifts to be a force for good beyond his forest. The light side is his incorruptibility.

Smeagle (Gollum, the infantile narcissist) is completely unconflicted in his selfishness. He wants the ring for his own gratification and will engage in any activity and betray any trust to possess it. He is the primitive power-God exem-plifying "Might makes right." His position is not romanticized by Tolkien, but serves as a clear moral parable warning of the dangers of egocentric power drives.

Aragorn (the king; the deity mystic) feels genuine fear at the thought of taking the ring because he distrusts his human capacity to be corrupted by power. He is the ultimate conformist who embraces the ancient wisdom of the sacred texts over his own impulses.

Sam (the faithful partner who actually briefly becomes a ring-bearer when he believes Frodo has been killed by the monster, Shelob) bears the Ring stoically and is protected from it's temptations by his total devotional love for Frodo. Deep committed love and service to others can cause us to have peak experiences of enhanced functioning, and Sam's brief stewardship of the ring is such a peak experience.

Faramir (the rationalist) sees that logically the best solution when he finds himself suddenly in charge of the ring bearer is trusting his most reliable sources of wisdom (Gandalf and the elves), and so goes against his father's wishes and refuses to take the ring.

Galadrial (a more than human mistress of subtle energies) laughs and briefly enjoys the fantasy of being the Goddess Empress of Middle Earth who is hopelessly loved by all. She has the integral felt appreciation for all points of view with diminished fear of death, and also the post-post-rational understanding of being a part of a larger energetic hierarchy. "And so Galadrial will fade away," she says with elegant equanimity.

Gandalf (the non-dual realizer) refuses the ring from a transcendent relationship with the infinite. His wisdom integrates rational, psychic, personal, and transpersonal energies, and he is Middle Earth's most reliable bridge between the material and spiritual realms.[10]

The beauty and maturity of these mythic figures informs us as to how to direct our own lives. From every worldview we can reach for and act from care and wisdom. The consistent decision to do so creates powerful coherent autobiographical narratives characterized by increasing compassion and depth of consciousness.

Let's examine reaching for mature transcendence with Teresa and her friend Sally (another public defender) who are out for shopping and lunch. They're taking a break at The Coffee Bean, and Sally is talking about her husband Henry:

Sally: "I can't believe I spent two hundred and fifty dollars for these boots. I can't tell Henry about it. He'll kill me."

Teresa: "You're kidding, right? You're not actually going to hide it from him? Eventually he'll notice you have new boots."

Sally: "I'll just tell him I got them on sale for forty dollars. He'll complain and then forget it."

Teresa: "But doesn't it bother you to lie to him?"

Sally: "He doesn't understand shopping, and he's happier to not know. As long as dinner is on time and we have sex once a week, Henry is fine."

Teresa: (She feels repelled, and yet it's also strangely appealing to take such a contemptuous attitude towards men. *"It's so easy for me to be contemptuous of John. I'm going to change that. He deserves honesty and respect and I can confront him without humiliating him."* She wants to say something positive to Sally but she doesn't want to join in on man-bashing.) "You and Henry seem happy together."

Sally: "As happy as you can be with a Mr. Clueless."

Teresa: (She laughs in spite of herself and feels guilty. *"What is it that Dr. Brown said, 'What's the internal representation beneath the feeling?' I guess I think it's cool to bad-mouth guys."*) "Sally, don't you think we get too down on men sometimes? I like Henry, and he seems to love you."

Sally: (She speaks blithely, without self-reflection.) "I'm just playing. Don't be so serious."

Teresa is feeling the myth of male incompetence that runs through her culture and is reaching for love and wisdom beyond it. She is acknowledging and tolerating her shame and using it to move her autobiographical narrative towards integrating thoughtless immature patterns into deeper love and wisdom. This is the same choice faced by all the Tolkien characters; choose the easier more selfish path, or struggle to be wise and caring.

The wisdom of what the hero knows, discovers, and cannot see.

In the Iliad, Cassandra was cursed to know what was going to happen and to never be believed by her contemporaries. From the outside of the myth we can see what the characters cannot and thus, like Cassandra, we yearn to warn and direct them even as they go to their predictable dooms. Most often their tragic flaws (their blind spots) involve refusing to face aspects of themselves because of pride and fear. Achilles' heel, the vulnerability that he denied and refused to adjust to, resulted in his death. Through self-reflection, dreams, meditation, study, and feedback from others, we can step outside our personal stories, see our tragic flaws and sacred gifts, and adjust our personal myths towards wisdom and compassion. We do not have to be fated (as were Achilles, Helen, Paris, Prometheus, Pandora, or Bluebeard's wives) to blindly act out the self-destructive aspects of our life stories, or (like Gilgamesh or Persephone) to not see our life's purpose until the end of our story. We can perceive, tolerate, and explore our pleasures and pains, enabling us to grow in our ability to discern and direct our life story, our personal myth, to serve love and wisdom. One of the major prices we often must pay to fully inhabit and direct our own myth is to be willing to recognize, feel, and effective process our shame emotions.

Autobiographical narrative from an interpersonal neurobiological perspective.

Daniel Siegal is the brilliant psychiatrist/neuroscientist who is the father of interpersonal neurobiology. He and his colleagues, contemporaries, and students have integrated neuroscience with attachment research in creating an empirical, science based understanding of individual and interpersonal health and development.[11]

Secure and Insecure Attachment Styles.

Attachment research demonstrates that a coherent autobiographical narrative, a life story that makes sense, is the strongest predictor of secure autonomous attachment in adults and secure attachment styles in their children.[12] Securely attached children (roughly 60%) get the loving attention they need most of the time, the separation they need most of the time, and are protected from psychological, physical, and sexual trauma. These kids tend to grow into secure autonomous adults whose lives make sense to them and whose relationships tend to be secure and relatively free from distortion.

Insecure attachment falls into three main categories, avoidant, preoccupied, and disorganized/disoriented.

Emotionally dismissive parents who are not sensitive to their children's needs for contact/separation tend to create avoidant attachment styles in children where emotions are suppressed, repressed, and/or denied.

Preoccupied parents have incoherent relationships with their own emotions, thoughts, and past experiences, and are capricious in their contact/separation with their children. Their relating style is run more from the parent's varying states of consciousness than in response to children's needs, and this tends to create ambivalent, anxious, clingy children who are insecure and hard to comfort.

Unresolved/disorganized parents (often terrifying or terrified) can allow or inflict psychological, physical, or sexual trauma on their children, which tends to result in disorganized/disoriented attachment styles. These kids can dissociate (space out) in response to the stresses of life, and routinely have distorted perspectives of themselves, others, and the world. Disorganized/disoriented attachment is usually accompanied by a more avoidant or ambivalent style.

A beautiful finding from attachment research is that attachment style can change if an individual can learn to make sense of their life. Children, teens, and adults who as infants demonstrated avoidant, preoccupied, or disorganized attachment styles (or who believed they did), *and then changed their status to a secure autonomous attachment style,* routinely report that they experienced at least one intimate relationship with a trusted other that helped them learn how to love.[13]

Interpersonal neurobiology.

Neurobiology has demonstrated that human brains are complex systems that grow through predictable stages *in relationship with other brains.*[14] Infants' brains are taught how to grow in relationship with caregivers' attention, gaze, love, touch, approval, and disapproval. All the forms of memory develop largely in relationship with other people. Implicit memory, which does not require focal attention and is constantly occurring without conscious awareness, begins in the womb in relationship with mother. Further, the default mode of our brain when we are not concentrating on anything in particular is to constantly scan the environment, especially the *social* environment.[15] Explicit memory, which does require focal attention and involves a conscious sense of something being remembered, comes on line at eighteen months when awareness of emotional separations and connections with mother dominate a child's worldview. The capacity for autobiographical memory includes a sense of life having a past, present, and future, matures at around five, and is informed by the increasing importance of feeling securely embedded in family culture. Autobiographical narrative in which we experience our self as a central figure in our unfolding life story is a progressive process of making sense of our interpersonal and intrapersonal relationships in past, present, and future. The more we experience ourselves as the active authors of lives that make sense in our relationships with others and ourselves, the more we inhabit secure autobiographical narratives.

The healthier we are (the more coherent our autobiographical narrative) the more resilient we are, which increases our abilities to tolerate stress without becoming lost in defensive states. When we exceed what Dan Siegal calls our "window of tolerance" for distressing emotion, we tend to cycle through *shame, humiliation, and rage*[16] (largely social emotions). Many researchers associate shame with feeling out of control, powerless, or helpless,[17] which all reflect forms of exceeding some window of tolerance for painful emotions, often involving real or imagined conflicts with others.

If shame can't be externally regulated, it is often avoided

The natural counter to shame's collapse is the approving gaze and touch of a caregiver, which is often not available. As toddlers and children, humans experience shame without mature abilities to effectively self-sooth and self-regulate, and so the shame emotions (including embarrassment, guilt, and humiliation) almost always evoke internal reflexes to avoid. The rage of the shame-humiliation-rage cycle influences us to attack others (external attacks) or ourselves (internal attacks). Internal attacks include depression, self-loathing, guilt, self-destructive actions, or negative distortions. External attacks include critical judgments, physical assault, contempt, or dismissal; all often manifestations of our early strategies to avoid threat and pain. *If left unexamined, unacknowledged, and unintegrated,* these habits of attack interfere with healthy growth and the development of a coherent autobiographical narrative, leaving us locked into identifying with wounds in our past, anticipating wounds in our future, and enduring distortions in the present moment.

FACES: Flexible, Adaptive, Coherent, Energized, and Stable.

Interpersonal neurobiology defines mental health as having an integrated brain. In an integrated brain, the mind (defined in interpersonal neurobiology as the process by which we direct energy and information flow) tends to be flexible, adaptive, coherent, energized, and stable.[18] Integration is blocked whenever we avoid feeling, acknowledging, and taking responsibility for anything we experience or do. This is the importance of feeling, understanding, and utilizing painful emotions in cultivating a coherent autobiographical narrative. As we do this we can reinterpret our past as a series of steps towards more love and compassion, develop hopeful and caring anticipations of our future, and be more fully present without distortion in the present moment.

John and Teresa are sitting in deck chairs at Hammonds Point in Santa Barbara, watching Teresa's son Aaron surfing a big west swell. John's daughter Ariel is at her mother's. It is a beautiful, clear, Santa Barbara winter day, and Teresa is describing her lunch with Sally:

> Teresa: "So when I told her that it's probably not good to bad mouth guys so much, she just blew me off."
>
> John: "I think that's beautiful."
>
> Teresa: (She turns towards John and asks incredulously,) "That she blew me off?"
>
> John: (Laughing.) "Of course not, silly. That you stood up for not bad mouthing men. It seems like ever since college and feminism it's been cool to trash guys. How are we going to raise strong, caring sons if men are considered messed up for just being men?"
>
> Teresa: (She's the mother of a son who is out surfing in front of them. She has participated in a lot of male bashing over her life and feels defensive.)

"What, you think women have it fair in our society? You think they haven't been suppressed, oppressed and exploited?"

John: (He cycles through shame and then anger; very much like a typical liberal middle class Anglo who is unexpectedly being called a racist.) "It's a nice day. Don't ruin it."

Teresa: "What do you mean, 'ruin it?' I didn't start going off with sexist crap."

John: "Come on. Why are you jumping on my case? You know what I think about all that."

Teresa: (Now she's confused. John is no sexist. To the contrary, he's been an advocate for every feminist cause she's ever been involved in. John has walked the walk from the bench in ruling against spousal abusers and exploitative employers. She looks down and blushes.) "I'm sorry. I don't know why I get so upset." (She has a sudden memory of her father yelling at her brother.) "Men can just be such jerks."

John: (He's gotten a hold of himself and recognizes the old defensive anger. He reaches for compassionate truth.) "I can't argue with that, but sick immature people hurt each other, men and women both. I don't like anybody being abused." (He reaches over and takes her hand.) "I know we agree on this." (She smiles, and at that moment Aaron comes running up, stoked.)

Aaron: "Did you see my last wave? I totally ripped."

Teresa: "No, but I'll take your word for it."

Aaron: "This kook chick cut me off. I don't know why girls go out on big days. They just get in the way."

John: (This is too perfect. He starts to laugh, as Teresa gets ready for a heated rebuke.) "You must be psychic, Aaron. You just said the perfect wrong thing."

Aaron: (He's a sharp, securely attached teen and gets right away what he did wrong. He speaks quickly before Teresa can let him have it.) "I'm sorry mom. I would have said the same thing if it was a guy kook."

Teresa: "You know how I feel about demeaning women. I don't want you to do it."

Aaron: (He gets it a little deeper.) "You're right. I was more down on her cause she was a girl. I don't know why it makes a difference but it does."

John: "Well at least we can talk about it."

Teresa: "John's right. I'm glad you get why it makes me mad." (Aaron smiles.)

Here is an attuned family that is supporting secure attachment styles and coherent autobiographical narratives in all members. John could have gotten lost in self-righteous defense of his integrity (preoccupied), Teresa could have surrendered to impulses to deliver an anti-sexist rant (unresolved/disorganized), or Aaron could have been too inhibited to share his (mostly) innocent sexism with his Mom and Step-dad (avoidant). Any of the three could have collapsed into self-loathing at their distortions or impulses to attack. Instead, they tolerated and examined their distressed feelings and looked for growth and insight. In the process each supported similar behaviors in other family members. Teresa woke up a little to her defensive, amplified fear of male abuse, John woke up a bit to his reflexive shame, anger, and impulses to attack when feeling unfairly accused, and Aaron examined his double standard for male and female kooks (a surfing term from the Hawaiian "kuk" or "shit" meaning a clueless beginning surfer).

This is how people create neural integration individually and interpersonally. They are flexible enough to change, adaptable enough to try new thoughts and behaviors, coherent enough to not lose attunement with self and others, energized by the excitement of life, and stable enough to not become rigid or lost in chaos. Each new perspective creates new neural networks that are more likely to appear in the future and are available to be included in more complex networks that can have a wider embrace of different perspectives. When this is the standard for individual and collective functioning, people create autobiographical narratives where they experience themselves as fully alive, directing their life story towards more love and health.

Autobiographical narrative from an Integrally informed perspective

Ken Wilber has illuminated a way of looking at the world that embraces multiple perspectives including the scientific, the aesthetic, and the moral.[19] He and his colleagues and students at the Integral Institute in Colorado advocate what they call Integral Life Practice (ILP), which involves attending to body/mind/spirit in self/culture/nature. ILP includes healthy food, exercise, rest, work, affiliation, spiritual practice, and study, as well as ongoing interest in deepening understanding and care of self and others. Out of the incredibly rich fabric of the Integral Operating System (so named because it can be used like a computer operating system to organize and synthesize multiple sources), a number of aspects of Integral theory are particularly relevant when dealing with autobiographical narrative. Three that we will explore are the ideas of horizontal health, vertical health, and shadow.

Horizontal Health

Horizontal health means being true to the worldview you are now occupying. For instance, in the example of Teresa's friends Sally and Henry, Sally felt a responsibility to have dinner on time and to be available for sex once a week. Within her worldview, it would be wrong to not do these things. Enhancing horizontal health is increasing our capacity to discern our current standards and best understandings and to be progressively more true to them. With Sally this would mean doing her best to do right as public defender, mother, wife, friend, and person *according to her current standards,* while including healthy activities and pleasures in her life that support her personally (like exercise, healthy food, church, shopping, and lunch with friends).

Vertical Health

Eventually, Sally might feel lonely or ashamed lying to Henry about how much things cost or speaking contemptuously about him, and it is no longer acceptable to rationalize these things away. At that point, *if she can tolerate her painful emotions and self-reflect on how they can teach and guide her,* she might shift her worldview towards thinking it's wrong to lie and demean Henry (and men in general), and right to be more honest and respectful with everyone. If she does this, Henry might respond well (as in, "Thank-you for trusting me with the truth,"), or badly (as in, "I can't believe you've been lying to me and running me down to your friends all these years.") Either way, she is expanding her worldview toward perspectives that involve deeper consciousness and more care. This is vertical health where we grow on different developmental lines towards greater compassion and depth of consciousness.

Development is include and transcend. If we inhabit new perspectives in healthy, wide-open ways that support integration of everything we experience and do, we never lose the habits, knowledge, and wisdom of previous worldviews; rather we expand to deeper abilities and a wider embrace. We *do lose previous worldviews* as our central organizing truths of existence because they have been supplanted with new worldviews that seem more valid to us aesthetically, morally, and empirically.

This conceptual developmental architecture of vertical health (validated by empiricism, phenomenology, structuralism, ethnomethology, and systems theory[20]) can empower us to make sense of all that we've ever been, with the understandings that there are new perspectives and abilities that we're growing towards. Knowing there are probably better understandings ahead doesn't diminish our current values. Even though there are certainly deeper, wider perspectives awaiting us in the future, the way to get to them is to fully embrace the truths and principles of now.

Anyone who is committed to both horizontal and vertical health is creating, sustaining, and enhancing a coherent autobiographical narrative where life makes sense in the past and present, and there is a sense of conscious direction towards a desirable and admirable future.

Shadow work

Shadow is simply those aspects of ourselves that we cannot easily perceive. A self-loathing adolescent girl who has no concept of how beautiful she is, a caring mother who feels inadequate and ashamed because she doesn't adore her difficult son one hundred percent of the time, or a gifted athlete who feels like a failure because he can't win every event, are all examples of people having difficulty perceiving and embracing positive aspects of themselves. A bully indifferent to the suffering his violence causes, a repressed, passive, sexually shut-down wife unaware of the rage she feels at her contemptuous husband, or a self-righteous crusader unwilling to examine his exploitative lascivious yearnings as he viciously attacks other's "sinfulness," are all examples of people who have difficulty perceiving forbidden or painful aspects of themselves.

One central tenant of Integral Life Practice is shadow work. Ken Wilber offers an elegant conceptualization of shadow as taking an aspect of "I" (for instance my shame), and making it a "you" (your "unacceptable behavior"), and ultimately an "it" ("Shameful behavior doesn't happen in this family"). Shadow work is transforming those "its" and "you's" back into "me's" and "mine" where I can own my shadow and integrate it into a healthy developing self.[21]

However it is done, shadow work involves recognizing that there are always facets of ourselves (both positive and negative) that we can't perceive, and that it serves us and others to cultivate curiosity and desire to gradually discover and integrate all our aspects. Since it is usually barriers of emotional pain that block our awareness of shadow (for example, barriers of fear, anger, or shame emotions that we learned to reflexively avoid as children), discovery and integration often begins with feeling, acknowledging, tolerating, and exploring pain. If we can cultivate curiosity about internal representations that sustain suffering, and reach for deeper wisdom and care, we can refine should-patterns into more mature, caring representations, and adjust our thoughts and behaviors to meet more refined standards, thus integrating shadow.

Since shadow is hard for us to see in ourselves, we often we need friends, colleagues, therapists, ministers, teachers, or family members to help us perceive shadow feelings and representations. This is why other's feedback is so important. A major problem is that critical feedback (*disapproval*) can evoke shame, humiliation, rage, anxiety, and thus defensive impulses to avoid self-awareness. When Teresa tentatively tried suggesting that they were too down on men, Sally dismissed her out of hand. Such bids quickly stop if met with dismissal or rejection (often experienced as disapproval).[22] Therefore it is of benefit to carefully consider the possible validity of any feedback no matter how uncomfortable it initially might be.

Shadow in action

Six months after Teresa, John, and Aaron's day at the beach, Aaron walks into the boys' bathroom at the local High School to find three guys (Blake, Sunny, and Jesse) doing a dope deal in the corner. Money and small packets are being exchanged. Aaron's first instinct is to leave, but he really has to go, and so he enters a stall and does his business. As he steps out, the three are facing him:

Jesse: "What are you looking at, loser?"

Aaron: "Nothing." (He tries to walk towards the door, but is blocked by Sunny.)

Sunny: "Not so fast. You have any money on you? How about that watch." (He grabs for Aaron's wrist.)

Aaron: (He pulls his wrist away.) "Come on, just let me go."

Jesse: "No way, bitch. Give us your money and that watch." (Aaron takes another step back. Teens tend to engage in more destructive activities in groups and Aaron knows he's in danger. Jesse gets more aggressive, and pushes Aaron against the wall.) "Give it up punk." (As Aaron refuses, Jesse becomes angry. *"Blake and Sunny gonna think I'm a pussy for letting this wimp fuck with me."* His story has become Aaron is humiliating him in front of his friends for not handing over the money and watch. He angrily slaps Aaron across the face and slams him back against the wall.)

Aaron: (His body feels weak in response to the shocking experience, but he breathes deeply and tries to think of the right thing to do. John has taught him to never engage in violence if at all possible but, if there is no other option, make it quick, brutal, and decisive. Figuring he has nothing to lose, he focuses on Jesse's sneering face, and hits him as hard as he can, breaking his nose, cracking his jaw, and loosening two teeth. Jesse falls down screaming, hitting his head on a sink, and Aaron darts out of the bathroom.)

Later that day John, Teresa, Aaron and Mr. Armstrong (the Dean of Students) are sitting in the Dean's office. Jesse is still in surgery at Santa Barbara Cottage Hospital with a broken nose, cracked jaw, and concussion, while Blake and Sunny are in custody. When Aaron ran out of the bathroom, he saw a teacher in the hallway, told him briefly what happened, and the other boys were caught before they could flush their crystal meth. Aaron is in shock from the encounter, and Teresa is overwhelmed that her son has sent another boy to the hospital. Jesse's parents have already threatened a lawsuit, while the police officer who interviewed Aaron at length finally concluded that Aaron had little choice but, "He shouldn't have hit the other kid so hard."

Mr. Armstrong: "I don't know what to do with you, Aaron. We can't allow violence at our school."

Aaron: "I'm sorry, he started beating me up."

Teresa: "You should have given him your money and watch. You might have killed that boy."

Aaron: "It wouldn't have made a difference. Those guys were mean." (She looks at him skeptically and he hangs his head.)

John: "Look, this is a horrible thing, but I'm proud of my son." (Teresa looks up, totally surprised.)

Mr. Armstrong: "Wait just a minute, sir. Jesse could have been killed. He has a concussion and is still in surgery. Don't you think this is a somewhat immature reaction?" (Mr. Armstrong's pluralistic, multicultural, non-hierarchical worldview does not have room for acceptable violence. The proper response to this kind of harm is moral condemnation.)

John: (The meaning of the whole drama comes together for him. He wants to honor all points of view, acknowledge the relativistic nature of appropriate action, and support his stepson's courage in a critical situation.) "I admire your zero tolerance for violence attitude on this campus. That's one of the reasons my children attend here. But my son was in an impossible situation in that bathroom, and I believe that under the circumstances he acted appropriately. You weren't there to protect him, so he had to protect himself."

Mr. Armstrong: "The other boys said that Aaron just hit Jesse in an unprovoked fashion."

John: "You've heard all the stories. Is that what you believe?" (Mr. Armstrong shakes his head and looks down, embarrassed for even mentioning that Aaron might be the original aggressor.) "Then he did exactly what I would have suggested under those circumstances. We all know that weak resistance just encourages bullies. He had to totally surrender to their violence or do violence himself. He didn't enjoy it. Aaron threw up in the hallway after he told the teacher what happened. If you feel you have to discipline him for protecting himself because your school couldn't adequately do the job, go ahead, but I'll appeal that decision all the way to the school board." (Teresa is speechless. She is adamantly against all forms of violence, but she trusts John at this moment. Aaron looks up at John gratefully. He's been in a nightmare of remorse since the episode. He keeps feeling waves of nausea remembering Jesse's nose breaking under his fist. Real violence, where harm is being delivered with deliberate angry intent, is shockingly horrible to those unaccustomed to it. He's been weak and depressed ever since the incident, which has added to his general sense of dread and shame.)

Mr. Armstrong: (He turns to Teresa.) "Surely you don't condone this?"

Teresa: "My family knows how much I hate violence, but I think my husband knows more about the male world than I do, and I support what he said. We'll process this in therapy, but I think it would be wrong for the school to penalize Aaron for protecting himself."

This story reflects a variety of aspects of horizontal health, vertical health, shadow, and autobiographical narrative.

Within the predominant high school worldview, Aaron's response to the bullying was appropriate and commensurate. It was a reflection of horizontal health. He wouldn't have chosen to do so much damage to Jesse but, when violence was offered to him, he had to decide what was consistent with his life story. According to his worldview, his choices were to allow himself to be victimized or act on the principle of never striking out unless there are no other options to personal injury, and then to fully commit. John taught him these principles (foundation aspects of the Warrior archetype), and later stood up for him in the face of considerable pressure.

After this traumatic experience, Aaron better understands the sickening flavor of such violence and is also more aware of the shifting nature of moral imperatives. He is more firmly committed to living a life by his principles even if it involves risk or trauma. This is vertical health where we discover new moral, behavioral, and relational perspectives, abilities, and nuances through embracing and processing our experiences and discovering that we need new refined perspectives to make sense of our expanding world.

Similarly, this is the first time that Teresa has deferred to John in a crucial parenting situation involving Aaron. This reflects her growing capacity to surrender to John's direction when he's being his best self; a huge shift for a woman who's life story was previously that she always had to take care of herself and her son independently, and could never trust a man's judgment over her own.

Meanwhile beneath the surface, shadow feelings and beliefs bubble in everyone in the room. All three adults are angry with Aaron and the other boys for this distressing incident, and are processing the painful scene through their defensive reactions.

Mr. Armstrong is angry with John for not collaborating with his pluralistic hypocrisy of taking a zero-tolerance stand against violence in an environment where sometimes the choice is do violence or be victimized. He is also frightened about the consequences to himself and the school from this ugly incident, ashamed that he somehow didn't prevent it, and unconsciously trying to make these distressing feelings and thoughts someone else's responsibility (turning "I's" into "you's") by blaming Aaron, the other boys, and John.

Teresa is confused. She feels unaccountably attracted to John's presence and power in dealing with a situation that she consciously finds repulsive. She's experiencing the unfamiliar enjoyment of offering devotional love to masculine integrity expressed through violence.

Aaron is depressed and ashamed but also secretly proud that he stood up to the "gangsters" who were trying to victimize him. This reflects the forbidden delight (simmering in everyone in the room) of a victim dominating an abuser and implementing martial law against bullies.

John is the only one so far to acknowledge a shadow pleasure at summary justice being done by admitting he's proud of his stepson. Simultaneously, he's repelled by the violence, angry at the school for somehow allowing it, and appreciative of the school for having a zero tolerance policy. While concerned for Jesse's health, he's also aware of his pleasure at a bully getting a comeuppance, but is wise enough to keep it to himself because he knows that any mention of it would immediately alienate both Teresa and Mr. Armstrong and put Aaron in an even more difficult position. At this moment John is having a peak experience of enhanced understanding of everyone's worldview in the room. This is partially due to being a judge for five years, which has developed his abilities to have appreciation for all points of view in emotionally or physically violent situations, and to the work he has done exploring, owning, and integrating shadow aspects of himself.

John's experience illustrates the power of an integrally informed approach when applied to autobiographical narrative. We can experience our life story as a process of accepting, owning and integrating all aspects of ourselves (especially our shadow which we resist perceiving). Such acceptance and integration leads to the horizontal expansion of exploring and being true to our current worldview, which ultimately creates vertical transformations into more inclusive, caring, wiser worldviews, which we can horizontally explore, be true to, expand into, and then transcend, and so on throughout our lives. Even as we are true to our current principles, we can be aware that they can probably be further refined into more mature values. We are not locked down into believing our life story is set in stone and cannot change. To the contrary, we can experience the rich possibilities of horizontal and vertical expansion that are available to all humans who have the courage to face shadow and grow.

1. Siegal (1999)

2. Siegal (2005)

3. Jung (1961)

4. Mushashi (1974)

5. Mitchell (2004)

6. Jung (1961)

7. Campbell (1949)

8. Watson (1956)

9. Wahoo (2005)

10. Tolkien (1954)

11. Siegal (1999)

12. Siegal (2005)

13. Siegal (1999)

14. Siegal (1999)

15. Siegal (2005)

16. Siegal (1999)

17. Nathanson (1987)

18. Siegal (2005)

19. Wilber (2006)

20. Wilber (2006)

21. Ibid

22. Gottman (2001)

9

Parenting Needs Shame

From *Days of Joy*

Here we sing, sitting round a fire
Some of us are young and some are old
I was just a babe, first in such company
Family never ends, it just flows on

These are days that might not come again
These are days of joy
These are days that we can share as friends
These are days of joy

These are days of joy, sun cascading down
We will keep the old songs alive
In the summer time

Nowhere is shame more misunderstood than in parenting. Most writers, researchers, teachers, and therapists relate to shame as the Great Enemy in parenting. The literature is full of such condemnations as in "It is wrong to shame our children," "Shame destroys children's sense of self," and "Critical attitudes in parents are destructive to children." Beneath the surface, the message seems to be, "Shame on you for shaming your children."[1] On the other hand, many writers (including John Bradshaw who popularized the idea of "toxic shame" in his books and lectures) assert that shame can guide us and be a source of spirituality.[2] The beauty of this message seems lost in an avalanche of loathing at shame's destructive influences. Let us face the evolutionary imperative that *shame emotions are as necessary to healthy development as joy, love, and approval.*

Any form of *unregulated* negative arousal is bad for our health. Pervasive anger has been associated with heart disease, poor judgment, and decreased immune

function, while pervasive fear can predispose individuals to distorted relationships, exhaustion, and chronic illness.[3] The ultimate parasympathetic collapse of
immobilization is our final organismic response to extreme trauma that we share
with all mammals. It can be compared to shame the same way extreme terror can
be compared to fear, and can actually result in injury through oxygen deprivation
since the reptilian part of our brain that drives immobilization only allows
enough oxygen to maintain a reptile rather than a warm blooded mammal.[4]
These negative effects are the result of *unregulated* anger/rage, fear/terror, or
shame/immobilization. Anger, fear, and shame *will* occur with our children. Terror, rage, or immobilization *can* occur with our children. We cannot prevent any
of these perfectly, and we wouldn't want to because self-regulating anger, fear,
shame, and trauma are necessary capacities for healthy living. We *can* help our
children learn how to optimally deal with negative arousal.

Approval and disapproval are the accelerator and brakes of development.

Family relationships (especially relationships with parents) are the foundation
sources of human socialization. These relationships are composed of intricate
intersubjective systems of non-verbal, verbal, and energetic communication.
Approval and disapproval are more or less constantly being expressed on all these
levels and are gradually internalized throughout childhood into a series of interior
representations (or "should-patterns") of how we believe we are supposed to be.
As detailed in Chapter Two, we instinctively monitor and react to our should-
patterns with interior approval and disapproval. A common response to either
interior or external disapproval is a shame emotion. The shame emotions are thus
as important in development as the brakes in a car. Sure, the accelerator is ener-
gizing, exhilarating and exciting, but we need the counterbalancing force of the
brakes or we will crash and burn.

Examples of people crippled by the inadequate development of shame emotions are psychopaths who use others as objects to attack for pleasure, sociopaths
who experience others as objects to utilize for personal gratification, and pathological narcissists who feel it is other's function to provide attention, appreciation, and other forms of narcissistic supply and who easily demean and withdraw
from those who don't.[5] Any of us can behave as if we have no shame if we are in
enough emotional pain and defensive activation that we lose empathy and
indulge in impulses to attack or flee with little or no concern for the suffering we
might cause. The shame emotions inform us when we are violating our personal
codes of existence and slap us on the wrist with discomfort, thus encouraging us

to adjust towards being more true to our principles. This system works great if we allow it. If we indulge defensive impulses to avoid experiencing, acknowledging, or acting on shame emotions we risk inflicting further damage to ourselves and others.

I believe that it is parents' *responsibility* to support the healthy development of the shame emotions by learning how to attune and optimally express approval and disapproval, and so gradually teach children how to self-regulate painful emotions in healthy ways. This helps children learn how to effectively utilize all painful experiences, especially the experiences they are most likely to defensively avoid.

The yin and yang of pleasurable and painful states.

All emotions and states of consciousness can have healthy and unhealthy manifestations. It's easy to see the healthy manifestations of the pleasure states such as love, joy, compassionate acceptance, bliss, deep relaxation, interest, attraction, and erotic polarity. It's also easy to see the unhealthy manifestations of the pain states such as sadness, shame, guilt, humiliation, anxiety, terror, resentment, and rage. It is harder to perceive the unhealthy manifestations of pleasure and the healthy manifestations of pain.

Every pleasure state can be a source of pathology. Lets briefly look at three; loving kindness, romantic infatuation, and joyful exhilaration:

- Loving kindness is an optimal attitude in most contemplative practices, but can be pathological if used to avoid feeling, acknowledging, or taking responsibility for emotions such as anger, contempt, fear, and shame, or impulses such as the urges to hurt another or ourselves. Meditators who attempt to "meditate away" their distress without first feeling and acknowledging their experience are essentially practicing dissociation (a defensive avoidance of self) rather than disidentification (a healthy differentiation and integration of self).[6]

- Romantic infatuation is a delicious feeling that boosts erotic polarity and intimate bonding but can also make us blind to a potential lover's shadow (their destructive aspects) through disengaging our mature capacities for interpersonal discernment.[7]

- Joyful exhilaration, if untempered by self-awareness of vulnerability, can lead to dangerous grandiosity as in the skier who is so intoxicated by the rush of his experience that he presses too hard and catastrophically crashes.

Similarly, painful states can be priceless sources of insight and self-knowledge. Anger tells us that we feel attacked by another and are probably having impulses to attack back or flee. Rage implies that old wounds have been restimulated, and we're probably having disproportionate impulses to respond, as in a road rage episode where one driver *has the impulse* to shoot another for cutting him off. Fear tells us that something dangerous might be occurring while terror (in the absence of a truly terrifying experience) implies that old, implicit memories of trauma have been restimulated. As illustrated by the examples in previous chapters, all the shame emotions can be priceless guides to self-reflection, self-awareness, and transcendence if acknowledged, explored, effectively processed, and assertively acted upon.

What's a parent to do? Shame parenting axiom #1: Talk to your children the way you want them to talk to themselves.

We tend to parent ourselves the way we were parented. Thus, each time a parent addresses a son or daughter, that parent is to some extent co-creating a voice that their child will hear internally throughout life. If I say "good girl" (verbally, non-verbally, or energetically) when my four-year-old daughter puts her toys neatly away, she's likely to feel a warm "good girl" feeling fifteen years later when she cleans up after herself. If I say "bad girl" (*either* verbally or non-verbally/energetically) when she creates a mess, she's likely to feel ashamed fifteen years later when she leaves a dirty kitchen for her roommates. This leads to Shame Parenting Axiom #1: *Talk to your children the way you want them to talk to themselves.*

Starting at around fourteen months, toddlers start having the capacity to experience shame with the accompanying impulses to seek emotional regulation through loving gaze, tone, and touch with primary caregivers. This is when parents begin more or less consciously to use (and teach) approval/disapproval to evoke and soothe shame emotions in service of socialization.

Children grow through worldviews that progressively include and transcend.

Children grow through stages of perspectives. Infants have no conscious awareness of past, present, and future, and don't seem to experience shame emotions. Normal toddlers are egocentric and experience shame when disapproved of, but only episodically feel internal disapproval for causing others suffering. Small children develop explicit memory and a sense of past, present, and future, and episodically feel shame emotions and adjust to "do right" while instinctively avoiding emotional pain through unconsciously developing a number of defensive strategies. Grade-schoolers want to follow rules to feel included in important social groups and tend to be very literal and doctrinal in their interpretation of rules (there's no cookies at five because it's against the rules rather than because eating them might spoil your appetite for dinner). Grade-schoolers can feel shame at violating rules when they have no other option (like being late because the car broke down), because the rules are sacred in themselves. Middle-schoolers are beginning to be able to hold competing concepts simultaneously and be able to rationally evaluate standards which they might reject if the standards seem unfair, unkind or not in keeping with peer norms. Each of these stages builds upon the others, and we never lose our capacities to temporarily inhabit any one of them. They include and transcend each other in a rhythm that continues throughout life with increasing conscious direction from the individual.

Different developmental stages involve different worldviews that respond optimally to different communication styles, which also progress in an include-and-transcend fashion. Infants who primarily need to be cherished grow into toddlers who need to be *additionally* contained and approved/disapproved of within a context of secure attachment. Small children and grade-schoolers *additionally* need rules clearly delineated and fairly enforced. Middle-schoolers and older teens *additionally* need rational explanations for why rules are made and how they are enforced.

Teen-to-adult children will always need to be cherished by parents, approved/ disapproved of by parents within a context of secure attachment, have clearly delineated boundaries, and want parents to provide rational explanations for family rules.

Knowing that children's worldviews grow through progressive stages helps us understand the *structure* of development, and guides us in formulating parenting *principles*. How our knowledge is applied on a moment-to-moment basis is the *process* of parenting. This process is enormously enhanced by parents' abilities to attune to themselves and their children.[8]

Attunement is feeling into yourself and others with caring intent.

Almost all healing/parenting/personal growth systems involve self-awareness and awareness of others with caring intent. I call this process *attunement*.[9] Attunement to self is attending to what you are feeling, thinking, and wanting with the intent of serving the highest good. Attunement to others is extending this process into considering what others might be feeling, thinking and wanting. Parental attunement is attuning to self and child with the responsibility to support family health *right now.*[10]

Consider the following dialogue between John's thirteen-year-old daughter Arial and her mother Annie. Arial spends alternate weeks at John and Teresa's house and at Annie's house with Annie's husband Morgan and their four-year-old daughter Karen. It's Saturday night and Annie and Morgan want to go out to dinner and a movie. Annie just got the call that the baby-sitter has food poisoning and must cancel and, for the first time, Annie is asking Arial to baby sit Karen:

Annie: "We'll only be gone for three or four hours. I'm leaving the numbers of the restaurant and the theater."

Arial: "Why do I have to? Get a baby sitter."

Annie: (She feels frustrated and urgent. It's 5:30, and the reservations at their favorite restaurant are for 6:00. Arial and Karen usually get along together wonderfully. She takes a deep breath and attunes to herself. *"I'm tense, impatient, and frustrated with Arial's anxiety."* She becomes aware of feeling guilty at pressuring her daughter. *"Why am I guilty? I guess I don't believe it's OK to give her stressful responsibility because she gets so anxious. Breathe, Annie, and relax. She needs to discover her strengths. Feel her."* As Annie extends her awareness into Arial, she imagines Arial, who tends to be a little obsessive, worrying about being solely in charge.) "Are you worried about the responsibility?"

Arial: (She visibly relaxes as her mother attunes to her. Feeling "felt" by another is a central characteristic of attuned communication, and is usually a reassuring experience.[11]) "What if something happens? What if she's a brat and I don't know what to do?"

Annie: (She feels more dialed in at this moment. Attuning to herself and her daughter has resulted in a shift from the frustrated urgent state she started the interaction with to a more compassionate and empathetic state. She also knows that Arial has spent most of the last eight years in a conformist worldview where black and white perspectives are what are most comprehensible and comfortable. She's currently transitioning into a more rationalist, relativistic worldview but, like most of us, tends to regress under stress. *"Give her clear instructions on what to do if there are problems. She can handle this better than she knows."*) "I will tell Karen that you are in charge and that she has to do what you say. If she causes problems, you can put her in her room for a ten-minute time-out. If something happens, you have the numbers of where we are. I'll also call before the movie to check in. You two love to hang out together, and you'll do fine. You'll have fun."

Arial: "Can we cook popcorn?" (Annie smiles and nods.) "And can we watch *The Little Mermaid?* Karen and I both like that video."

Annie: "Just nothing R-rated." (Arial laughs. This is a private joke because Arial hates R-rated movies.) "Let's go talk to Karen."

This example started with a mother and daughter in defensive states. Annie was urgent and frustrated with her daughter's lack of adult confidence. Arial was anxious and catastrophizing about an activity (hanging out with her sister) that she had done hundreds of times with Annie or Morgan in the house. Annie felt into herself with positive intent, felt her defensive state, soothed herself, and remembered that she was dealing with a thirteen-year-old's worldview. She then attuned to Arial with the intent of serving the highest good, which she determined was having the date with Morgan while Arial took on a new responsibility of babysitting her little sister. Annie used the parental attunement process to understand, support, and guide her daughter to become more competent and caring.

Shame parenting axiom #2: When attuning, explore shame emotions.

Attunement is difficult when we are in defensive states because defensive states resist self-reflection and empathy. This leads us to shame parenting axiom #2: *When attuning, explore shame emotions.* Annie noticed her guilt at asking Arial to baby sit and, *instead of avoiding it* by not going out, frantically calling for other help, or attacking Arial with coercion or demands, *she explored it* by looking for the internal representations, the should-patterns, she was violating, and then making an informed decision on what served the highest good. She became self-aware of her should-pattern that she should not cause Arial anxiety if she could help it, and adjusted to realizing that resilience is created by successfully taking on manageable problems. This "inoculation" process cultivates confidence, courage, and growth, which are all hallmarks of resilience.[12]

Since we all have reflexes to avoid feeling, acknowledging, and processing shame emotions, shame parenting axiom #2 is easier said than done. The bottom line in families is that the buck stops with parents. Healthy families are power hierarchies with caring parents at the top and children, in-laws, and others lower down. Parents, like CEO's in companies, determine the culture of the family (safe or unsafe, warm or cold, open or closed) and are ultimately responsible for setting boundaries, creating rules and guidelines, and supporting everyone's health and development (including their own). If this involves painful or effortful work, then it's a parent's job to get the support they need, develop the skills they require, and take the risks necessary to optimize love and health in their family.

Shame parenting axiom #3, approve of the child, disapprove of the behavior or perspective.

If my two-year-old son is beating on my car with a hammer, I'm going to disapprove and let him know with my voice, words, posture, and touch that he has violated an important rule of respecting property. In response he might feel the parasympathetic slump of shame, leaving me the option of helping him regulate that emotion by attuning to him and providing the love and boundaries he needs (in this case understanding and care while taking the hammer away). He also might cycle through shame to humiliation and rage at my censure, creating the necessity for me to set different boundaries (containing his impulses to do emotional or physical violence by constraining him or giving him a time out) which, when he eventually is emotionally accessible, can be processed to enhance his current understanding (horizontal health) and to expand his perspectives (vertical health). You might have noticed that this sequence is used throughout this book repetitively for similar behaviors at many ages, adjusted for worldview, type of boundary, and content of the parental message. The theme is the same; attune to self and child, and selectively approve/disapprove of behavior while always approving of the person. Why is this sometimes so hard for parents? Four major sources of difficulty are **contempt, fusion, disengagement, and codependence.**

Contempt

Contempt is a form of emotional violence that involves angry critical judgments of another or ourselves. As parents it is often easy to be contemptuous of a child engaging in behaviors that we personally find despicable. This contempt tends to amplify the more we believe that he or she has the knowledge and ability to choose healthier options. Consider the difference between your two-year-old son beating on your new Lexus with a hammer, and your sixteen-year-old son doing the same. We expect the sixteen-year-old to have much more knowledge that the behavior is wrong and to have enormously more self-control to choose better options of regulating hurt, angry emotions.

If contempt is indulged ("My son/daughter deserves my contempt because …"), it effectively blocks attunement. We can't accurately feel into ourselves with healing intent while indulging destructive impulses. We don't want to because we're likely to feel ashamed of who we are or what we're doing if we become consciously aware of our ugly attitudes and behaviors. Similarly, contempt effectively blocks attunement to others because all emotional or physical violence involves blocked empathy. The ability to reflexively cut off empathy and engage in necessary violence was a reproductive advantage to our hunter-gatherer forebears but, when warped into serving our defensive patterns, blocked empathy can cause unnecessary violence and suffering.

Contempt communicates a dismissive attitude and promotes toxic shame where the painful emotion is unnecessarily prolonged. Contempt compromises effective communication and self-reflection and elicits defensive reactions. The energetic message is, "It doesn't matter what you do, I find *you* contemptible." How can anyone respond productively to this message? Imagine someone finds you contemptible. Your initial reaction is probably not, "Yes, you are right. I am a contemptible person." To maintain any sense of integrity of self, this message must be resisted. Predictably, "You are contemptible," will usually elicit defenses such as denial, rationalization, projection, and active and passive aggressive attack.

The *experience* of contempt, and *impulses* to indulge contemptuous perspectives, can be productively processed in the same ways we've explored for other painful emotions. If I am contemptuous of you, what should-pattern do I experience you violating? What is a more compassionate and mature perspective for what is happening at this moment? What serves the highest good for everybody right now? Any emotion or impulse, including contempt, so processed tends to create more love and growth.

Fusion

Fusion involves identifying to an unhealthy extent with a child's activities, happiness, successes, failures, or life in general. The soccer mom who screams at the coach for not giving her daughter playing time, the father who insists that his son join the football team when the boy would rather play flute in the band, the mother who obsesses about her daughter's prom dress and popularity, or the parents who can't stand it that their son is not making more friends in his second grade class, are all examples of fusion. Attunement is not possible when you're so connected or invested that you can't supportively feel into what another is feeling, thinking or wanting. If the above parents were doing this with their children, Soccer Mom might discover that her daughter is embarrassed by Mom's outbursts, Football Father might find that his son has deep purpose playing the flute and dislikes football, Prom Dress Mother might discover her daughter feels coerced by Mom's needs for her to be beautiful and popular, or Socially Anxious Parents might find that their second grader is happy with his one good friend, and doesn't particularly yearn for more. These parents need help in attuning to themselves and their children so they can learn to discern where parents stop and children start. This attunement/discernment tends to naturally support a child's personal life path rather than a fused parent's idealized vision of how their child should be.

Disengagement

Disengagement is avoiding participation in a child's life. The father who never goes to parent conferences, the mother who never talks about problems, and the parents who set no boundaries and allow destructive behaviors are examples of disengagement. Children feel abandoned by disengaged parents, and abandonment often leads to shame emotions and the avoiding strategies for dealing with shame emotions. Children exhibiting chronic overeating, withdrawal, too much T.V, drugs/alcohol, destructive acting out like shoplifting or vandalism, or abusive oppositional behavior often have a disengaged parent.

Disengaged parents can be cut off from their own feelings, thoughts, and impulses (often exhibiting a dismissive attachment style). If you cannot attune to yourself, your ability to attune to others will be severely compromised. These parents need help in discerning, self-reflecting, and relating in cleaner more productive ways with themselves and their children. This often involves having to address their own blocks to awareness of feelings. Beneath these blocks can be shame in response to unrealistically harsh internal representations, often involving a subjective sense of failure to live up to impossibly high standards.

Codependence

Codependence is taking inappropriate responsibility for another's actions. When I studied Transactional Analysis, codependence was often defined as persecuting or rescuing. A therapist/minister friend of mine, Denton Roberts, once defined a "rescue" as promising to deliver goods you can't deliver. Persecuting is pretending that attacking another will help with a chronic problem. If a mother addresses her son's alcoholism by dumping out his bottles, she's pretending that dumping bottles helps his alcoholism. If a father continually tolerates his daughter's reckless promiscuity and believes that his acceptance will help her be healthier, he's avoiding dealing with her sexual acting out. If parents make it their job for their teen son to keep track of, accomplish, and check his homework, they are pretending that they are empowering his sense of adult responsibility while actually enabling him to stay disorganized and incompetent. If a father beats his son for lying, he is pretending that physical abuse will address his son's dishonesty. All these persecuting and rescuing behaviors are forms of codependence which involve parents participating in a problem while pretending to positively address it.

Usually the parental work in identifying and resolving codependence is to get support from friends, family, groups, teachers and/or therapists to discern impulses to rescue or persecute. These impulses are often driven by shame at not having a child live up to a parent's internal representations of how *my* family should be. As parents learn to discern their own codependence, they can identify and set clean boundaries that are healthy responses to unhealthy behaviors. In the above examples, the alcoholic teen's mother could go to Alanon, seek therapy, and possibly arrange an intervention to hospitalize her son. The father of the promiscuous girl could insist on family therapy. The parents of the passive teen could refuse to do his homework, let him fail or pass on his own, and seek help from friends, church/temple, school, therapists, or trusted relatives as the son learns that Mom and Dad will no longer take responsibility for his failure or success. The physically abusive father could enter anger management, AA if he has a drinking problem (common with physical abuse), or seek other forms of psychotherapy to explore his violence with the goals of self-regulation and opening up his family to new perspectives.

When children try to unilaterally choose love in unhealthy family systems, they usually develop codependence. This makes sense developmentally. The roles the child has access to in such systems are attacking self (such as going crazy, developing addiction, suicide, or failing), attacking others (such as being snotty, oppositional, violent, bullying, or self-righteously judgmental), deserting the family (as in running away, "adopting" a friend's family, or becoming completely lost in a middle school or high school teen culture), or trying to save the family by being a self-sacrificing codependent. Common codependence examples are the girl who puts her drunk mother to bed, the boy who makes excuses for the bruises left by his abusive father, the daughter who always takes responsibility for family problems, or any child who has no awareness of personal yearnings and/or assumes he/she has no right to articulate personal needs.

The family shame daisy chain

Often, when one family member responds inappropriately to shame, another family member is cued to have a complementary defensive response, which can cue *another* family member's complementary response, and so on until a *parent* can attune and respond appropriately. A parent needs to take responsibility for this process since parents are at the top of the family power hierarchy, and thus determine the family culture. A child can attune first and begin a healing process, but it is not the child's *responsibility* to be the first to attune in a healthy family. If a child's role is to be the one primarily responsible for regulating the family's emotional balance, then that child probably has a codependent defensive pattern within the family, which the parents are either encouraging or tolerating. On the other hand, when anyone attunes and creates caring connections, it can have a positive daisy chain effect resulting in love rippling through the system.

Let's look in on Arial and Karen. They played happily together for almost three hours before there were any problems. It's now 9:30 which is an hour past Karen's bedtime. Arial has never had to put Karen to bed, and so has been easily put off by "Let's watch Aladdin" and "Can we make more popcorn?" Meanwhile, both girls are getting tired and cranky. The last half hour Karen has been driving Arial crazy by repeatedly asking, "When is Mommy coming home?" Arial has been laboring heroically to be a responsible baby sitter, but she's beginning to feel anxious herself about Mommy and Morgan:

Karen: (The more tired she is, the more whiney her voice becomes.) "When's Mommy coming home?"

Arial: "I already told you. Soon. Now, get your PJ's on."

Karen: "No! I want Mommy to do it."

Arial: "Well Mommy's not here, so let me help."

Karen: "No! I want Mommy!"

Arial: (*"They'll be mad if Karen isn't in her pajamas. She's such a brat sometimes."*) "Don't be such a brat. It's time to get ready for bed."

Karen: (She hears the contempt and disapproval, and cycles quickly through shame, humiliation and into rage.) "I'm not a brat. You're a brat. I'm going to tell." (She starts to cry, runs over to the popcorn, and throws it on the floor.) "You're a brat!"

Arial: (She feels desperate. Her obsessive anxiety is already imagining horrible humiliating condemnation from Morgan and her Mom. Morgan is very protective of Karen and has often blamed Arial when Karen gets upset. As tears of frustration run down her face, she snaps.) "*Shut up*, Karen! You *are* a brat and you've made a mess. You have to help clean it up." (At this moment the door opens as Morgan and Annie come home from a nice date to find two screaming, crying girls standing in the middle of a huge mess of spilled popcorn.)

Annie: (Happy from her date, this scene blindsides and deflates her. *"I should have cancelled. I thought Arial could handle this. I can't do anything right."*) "Arial! Don't yell at your sister."

Morgan: (*"I knew we couldn't trust Arial to be responsible."*) "Arial what's going on?"

Arial: "I tried to get Karen to go to bed and …" (Karen cuts her off.)

Karen: "She called me a brat."

Morgan: "We don't call people names in this house." (His voice takes on some contempt.) "You *know* that Arial." (She cringes away from his tone.)

Annie: (*"I called three sitters, and I thought the girls would be fine together."* She notices Morgan glaring at Karen. *"I hate that tone Morgan's using."*) "Come on Morgan, you don't know the whole story. It's late and nobody's hurt. I think Arial did a good job."

Morgan: (He was feeling a nice romantic glow from dinner out and a good movie. His current perspective is that Arial has been bullying his biological daughter and has wrecked the evening. There are significant differences in the emotional charges that parents have for stepchildren and biological children. Relative emotional connection in a family tends to be a taboo subject, and stepparents (like adoptive parents) often have unrealistic should-patterns about how they should "feel just the same" about all the children. It's easy to be ashamed at not living up to such internal representations. The reality is that every child has a different family experience, and stepparents usually *do* feel differently towards stepchildren. One telling statistic is that a stepfather is *one hundred times* more likely than a biological father to sexually abuse a stepdaughter. Morgan is a good guy who doesn't engage in sexual or physical abuse, but sometimes the subtleties of family dynamics elude him; especially late at night after splitting a bottle of wine at dinner. He feels challenged now by Annie and responds sarcastically.) "What do you mean, 'good job?' Making a mess and calling Karen names?" (Arial is now crying so hard she can't talk.)

Annie: (During her first marriage, John never raised his voice to her or Arial, and Morgan rarely does. She's also tired, disappointed that a romantic night has been cut short (she was secretly planning to seduce Morgan when they got to bed), and she too is a little foggy from the wine they had with dinner. Feminine people are usually sensitive to subtle energies, and Annie feels the discrepancy between Morgan's connection with Karen and Arial. Though she usually doesn't blame him for it, she feels extra protective on those rare occasions that he seems unreasonably critical of Arial. She explodes.) "Don't you dare take that tone with me or Arial! Get out of here right now. I'll talk to you later. Right now *our children* need attention, not you being *mean.*" (Morgan realizes he's screwed up and feels mortified. He tries to apologize to Arial, but she's hysterical. Annie takes charge while still furious at her husband.) "Just stop, Morgan. We'll talk later. Girls, go to your rooms. Everything's fine now. I'll clean up the mess. You two did great staying home with each other."

Morgan: (His face feels hot. *"She's right. I'm being a jerk. Arial's barely thirteen, and it's way too late for Karen to be up. Do something to help."*) "I'm sorry you guys. I'll clean up the popcorn." (Annie looks at him gratefully as she hustles the girls off to get ready for bed.)

Annie: "Arial, why don't you take a nice warm shower? I'll put Karen down and then I'll kiss you good-night." (Arial is still sniffling but nods and goes off to shower. Annie picks up Karen and hugs and kisses her as she walks into her room.) "Let's get your pajamas on."

Karen: (As she puts on her pajamas, she remembers her temper tantrum with Arial and she feels distressed.) "Mommy, I wouldn't put my PJ's on and Arial got mad at me, so I threw the popcorn on the floor."

Annie: (She's attuned to her daughter and can feel her shame. She speaks to her emerging worldview of identifying and being true to the rules, while simultaneously loving and cherishing her.) "Do you think you made a mistake, especially after I told you to do what your sister says?" (Karen nods her head.) "Do you want to apologize before you go night-night?"

Karen: (She likes this idea because she loves her sister and feels guilty for contributing to the mess.) "Let's tell her right now." (They walk into the other room where Arial is emerging from the shower in her robe. Karen hugs her.) "I'm sorry I didn't do what you said. I'm sorry I threw the popcorn on the floor."

Arial: (She has no problem with Karen, but she's still mad at Morgan. The apology makes her feel better about how everything was a mess when her parents got home.) "That's OK. I'm not mad at *you.*" (Morgan, sensing there is a reconciliation going on, walks in.)

Morgan: (He knows he has a tendency to rationalize bad behavior. *"Just apologize. Don't justify."*) "I'm sorry Arial. You did great taking care of Karen and I shouldn't have gone off on you."

Arial: "You didn't even listen to my side."

Morgan: (*"What do you expect? I walked in on you two yelling and making a mess. Stop it, Morgan! Make it safe for her to be mad. Besides, she's right. You didn't listen to her side.*) "You're right sweetheart. You are so mature that I forget it's hard to do things like baby-sit your sister for the first time. I'll bet you two had fun most of the night."

Karen: "We watched *The Little Mermaid,* and *Aladdin.* Arial made popcorn."

Morgan: (He smiles ruefully.) "Yeah, I saw the popcorn." (Everybody laughs and goes to bed. Much mollified, Annie goes back to plan one and initiates lovemaking.)

This scene started off with a negative shame daisy chain. It kept accelerating until a parent (Morgan, who felt into himself and then other family members) was able to attune and start a positive daisy chain. It wasn't just his offer to clean up the popcorn that helped turn things around, but rather his entire energetic shift to taking responsibility for creating love instead of hurt with Annie and the kids. Like most healthy families, when one parent started attuning, it got progressively easier for everyone else to move towards love. Healthy families are usually characterized by parents who practice attunement regularly. In this case a variety of positive adjustments became possible as Morgan and Annie began feeling into themselves and others with positive intent:

- Annie initially distrusts Morgan when he's coming from a destructive place, but never looses connection with him. She feels it immediately when he shifts into being present and caring, and starts trusting him again.

- Karen's four-year-old worldview needs to process the upsetting situation from a black and white mythic perspective. Like many four-year-olds, she believes her parents have God-like powers, and she relaxes when they use their authority to bring justice and caring back through the mediums of compassionate understanding, acceptance, articulating rules, and giving clear direction.

- Arial's emergent rational worldview needs fairness to be served, and wants deeper understanding of the unique qualities of the situation; all of which she eventually receives from her parents.

- Annie and Morgan hurt each other in the exchanges, but they keep reaching for attunement. Neither one lets a difficult episode spoil a good night.

Everyone felt some shame emotions and defensive impulses to avoid them. Annie and Morgan attuned first to themselves (they felt, acknowledged, and reflected on their experiences, reaching for optimal perspectives and behaviors), and then attuned to each other and their children, creating meanings and interventions that were consistent with the girls' worldviews. As a result everybody practiced healthy self-regulation, and everybody's autobiographical narrative made a little more sense. Everybody's worldview was positively stretched a tiny bit, reflecting the value of using parental attunement to feel and process shame emotions in service of love.

1. Middelton-Moz (1990), Nathanson (1987), Kaufman (1980), Gilbert (2002)

2. Bradshaw (1990)

3. Shore (2003)

4. Porges (2006)

5. Masterson (1981)

6. Wilber (2006)

7. Deida (1997)

8. Witt (2007)

9. *Ibid*

10. *Ibid*

11. Siegal (1999)

12. Shore (2003)

10

Marriage: Shame Heals and Destroys

From *Judge and Jury*

When charged with loving you
I'll take a guilty plea.
Your compelling evidence
drives me to my knees.
Oh, can you hear me now,
you're my last appeal, so let's make this deal:
Oh, if you let it go
we'll waltz away and open you to God,
Just let us waltz away and open you to God

You are my judge and jury,
you can't object, I am innocent.
Show me your suffering,
I'll pass this test
or die my love.

Four years after Teresa divorced him, Preston began a secret affair with a married woman from work named Alice who eventually left her husband for Preston. Tonight they've gone to a party at their friend Randle's house and both have had a few drinks. Preston and Randle have also smoked a joint in the back yard. At the party there's a mixture of couples and single adults who are all mingling and drinking:

Preston: (He approaches an attractive blond woman in a low cut red dress.) "Nice dress. I'm Preston. I haven't seen you here before."

Amy: "I'm Amy. I'm a friend of Randle's sister."

Preston: "I didn't know Ellie hung out with such beautiful women."

Amy: (She laughs at the obvious come on.) "You don't waste any time do you?"

Preston: (He smiles charmingly.) "Life is short, baby."

Amy: "Isn't that a wedding ring?"

Preston: "A marriage is what you make it. My wife and I have an understanding." (He hasn't noticed that Alice has quietly walked up behind him while he's hitting on Amy.)

Alice: "Yeah, we both understand that you're an asshole." (The night proceeds to get progressively worse for Alice and Preston.)

Meanwhile, Teresa and John are finishing dinner across town. Aaron is out with a friend, and Arial is at Annie and Morgan's:

John: "It's your turn to do the dishes."

Teresa: "Just once I'd like you to just do them instead of remembering whose turn it is."

John: "I'm only trying to make things fair."

Teresa: "I know but sometimes fair is …" (She struggles to express some indefinable feeling.) "… boring."

John: (This especially hurts because he's been accused of being boring at one time or another by most of the women he's been intimate with.) "I just don't get it. I do my best to do things right, and you get mad at me."

Teresa: "I'm not mad. I'm bored. I want something more exciting or romantic."

John: "Romantic like doing the dishes for you?"

Teresa: "Now you're being sarcastic." (This leads to a thirty-minute, laborious conversation where they end up agreeing that Teresa likes pleasant surprises and John has trouble creating them. During this tedious talk, John feels ashamed for not being a more exciting husband, and Teresa feels ashamed for not being as attracted to her husband as her internal representations say she should be.)

Unconditional love is largely a myth

Marriage is the most conditional intimacy there is. A spouse wears more relational hats than any other person in our lives. Our parents can care for us, our
friends can relate with and support us, we love and are loved by our children, our
dog is relentlessly loyal to us, but only spouses are lovers, friends, caregivers, and
family members all in one. If one of these channels suffers, the whole relationship
suffers. A spouse has multiple roles including lover, friend, support source, co-
parent, and embodiment of masculine presence or feminine love. Both partners
suffer when either spouse doesn't step up to their responsibilities to create love
and process shadow *in any marital role.*

Shame begins as a social emotion. A caregiver's look of disapproval can cause
an energized child to collapse into shame. This reflects a sudden shift from activation in the sympathetic branch of the autonomic nervous system to activation of
the parasympathetic branch. As children mature, shame is elaborated into the
shame family of emotions including guilt, embarrassment, inferiority, and humiliation among many others. These emotions can arise from experiencing disapproval in *any relationship* we have with *others* and/or *ourselves* in the *present, past,*
or *future* in *reality* or *fantasy.* For example, an individual can fantasize engaging in
secret forbidden behavior in the future, and feel shame, even though no one else
is involved and the behavior has not (and perhaps never will) occur. The shame
emotions are so omnipresent that they can be brought to bear in practically any
situation.

Since a marriage has such central importance and involves a wider range of
roles than any other relationship, it has the most potential interpersonal impact
on our developing adult abilities to process and integrate shame. A demeaning
spouse can drive us deeper into shame emotions when they arise. This creates an
unsafe context, which is a recipe for strengthening defensive habits to avoid productively tolerating and processing distress. A clueless spouse (like the wife of a
tax evader who never questions his financial maneuverings) can conspire with her
partner to ignore self-destructive perspectives and impulses. A self-aware compassionate spouse can influence her partner to examine, tolerate, accept and integrate
painful material, and thus enhance health and accelerate personal and relational
development. This kind of attuned partner feels a sense of responsibility to create
love and process shadow in herself and to support those capacities in her partner.
Creating love and processing shadow often require abilities to feel, tolerate,
explore, and act on shame emotions. Let's examine how these principles are
reflected in the above two marriages:

Preston is technically a great lover. When sex starts he confidently tunes into his partner, breathes her breath, feels into her body, and guides her to increasing levels of erotic bliss. Since he is primarily an egocentric first stage man, he does this mostly for himself because (as a masculine person) he gets off on feminine pleasure. One of Teresa's main passive aggressive attacks on him towards the end of their marriage was to stop enjoying their lovemaking. This infuriated Preston who prided himself on being a great lover, and he felt demeaned and deprived by her lack of pleasure. Rather than using her shut-down as a cue that something was wrong with the way he was loving her, he made it a rational for more blatant cheating and lying. Preston has some capacity to care for others but, when given an opportunity for personal pleasure that might also hurt someone else (for instance infidelity or drug/alcohol abuse), he's likely to collapse into self-gratification and ignore the inner voices that are trying to help him grow. He is not a sociopath. He loves Alice and Aaron, and generally behaves ethically in his business. He feels tingles of guilt and shame when he transgresses, but has practiced avoiding such signals by focusing exclusively on what he currently wants and *never* tolerating or processing shame emotions. He is contemptuous of self-reflection, therapy, and all forms of spiritual practice, while embracing cynicism (which supports his egocentric worldview and fears of self-discovery).

Alice is Preston's reciprocal in many ways. We tend to attract, be attracted to, and marry people who have dreams and wounds that complement our own dreams and wounds.[1] Alice's first husband was a loyal, faithful guy who bored her. She has always assumed that she's special and deserves special treatment. As a high school senior she was shocked when she was "only" elected Prom Princess and not Prom Queen. When Preston first seduced her she welcomed his attention and felt entitled to cheat on her husband.

The argument that began at the party accelerated later that night to Alice throwing dishes at the wall and Preston sleeping on the couch, but nothing much changed. He was angry with her for "overreacting," and she with him for being a "dog," but the next morning when they made love and Preston told her she was the best, she believed him and felt better. Both blamed the alcohol for their fight, and neither took personal responsibility for the wounds in their marriage that created the incident. Preston didn't examine the tingles of guilt, shame, and humiliation that he barely felt and automatically suppressed while being caught red-handed propositioning Amy and demeaning Alice. Alice didn't examine the subtle shame of indulging in violent emotional attacks, or have any curiosity about her wildly fluctuating perspectives of Preston (sometimes she saw him as an angel, sometimes as a devil, but never as both simultaneously). Their marriage seems at least partially a conspiracy to help each other *not grow* either horizontally or vertically, while also creating absorbing negative drama that results in unnecessary suffering for lots of people.

Teresa was profoundly unhappy in her marriage with Preston. She couldn't stand Preston's collapses and selfish dishonesty, so she left him and eventually married **John** who was an honest, earnest, and occasionally passive-aggressive man she could trust. Where Preston and Alice are somewhat selfish first stage partners, John and Teresa are mostly caring, egalitarian second stage partners who genuinely want to serve each other and the world. They believe in total honesty, fairness, and caring. Their suffering is caused largely by difficulties they have in moving through shame emotions to deeper truths. Through therapy and other forms of personal growth and exploration, they are learning to support increasingly wider acceptance of everything, and steady integration towards John being the embodiment of pure consciousness, and Teresa the embodiment of pure love. John's awkwardness with masculine/feminine polarity has always irritated Teresa, and Teresa's contempt at his embarrassment has always felt emasculating to John. Unlike Preston and Alice, Teresa and John not only go to therapy, they *enjoy* therapy. Self-reflection and increased care feels beautiful, good, and true to both of them. Here is the session they had with Dr. Theo Brown after their dishes argument:

John: "Another dumb argument."

Teresa: "You mean you think *I'm* dumb."

John: "That's not what I said."

Teresa: "It is what you mean, isn't it?"

Dr. Brown: "How attracted to each other are you right now?"

John: "What?"

Teresa: "That's not what we're talking about."

Dr. Brown: "Exactly."

John: (These cryptic references are irritating. It also evokes a sense of failure and incompetence when someone seems to see something he can't.) "Come on. Just say what you think. Why do you have to be so mysterious?" (Teresa nods in agreement and looks expectantly at Theo.)

Dr. Brown: "I want to help you ask yourselves the right questions when you're in pain. It seems that being right, or who remembers the best, or being fair becomes more important than, 'Am I loving well right now?'"

Teresa: (Unconsciously shifting into a self-righteous tone.) "We believe in good communication."

Dr. Brown: "I thought you wanted to feel less bored and more loved."

Teresa: "Isn't good communication the way to do that?"

Dr. Brown: "It depends how you define 'communication.' Tedious boring talk can establish safety, but I think you two are able to trust enough to move beyond safety to facing your own demons and creating love. When you are distressed with each other, what's the one part that bugs you the most?"

John: "That we're mad instead of caring." (Teresa nods in agreement.)

Dr. Brown: "So how do you best evoke caring in yourself and Teresa?"

John: "I get it. Not by arguing about who's right, what's fair, or who screwed up."

Teresa: "I get so sick of those talks."

Dr. Brown: "And yet they keep happening. There are quicker ways to love. Discerning your contribution to the problem and acknowledging it, searching for what's valid about the other's point of view, and adjusting *right now* is more attractive than tedious processing. Try it." (John looks confused, but Teresa, in this protected environment, wakes up a little and smiles at John. Therapy has been referred to as a "safe emergency" where scary stuff can be handled in a secure context.[2])

Teresa: "I love you baby. I know I can be a demanding bitch."

John: (He remembers discussing with Theo how women like to be claimed.) "Yeah, but you're *my* bitch, and when you demand love you deserve it." (They both start laughing, visibly attracted.)

Dr. Brown: "That's what I'm talking about."

Shame marital axiom #1:Your state of consciousness evokes similar and/or complementary states in your spouse.

When two people look into each other's eyes, mirror neurons in their brains recapitulate the other's *state of consciousness, including intentionality.*[3] In addition, our brains reflexively scan the environment and constantly evaluate whether we are safe or in danger. Attraction/repulsion, approval/disapproval and yum/yuck are primary emotional reactions that are always operating and contributing to our states of consciousness. This is called elaborative appraisal by neuroscientists and is the first level of emotional reaction we have to most everything. If your spouse looks at you with repulsion/disapproval/yuck, you will empathetically *feel* this state and instantly react. Feeling their anger/contempt/disapproval is likely to immediately evoke some variant of shame-humiliation-rage in you with accompanying impulses to avoid threatening material by attacking, denying, rationalizing, projecting, dissociating, or other defensive strategies. Awareness of these processes is invaluable in establishing and maintaining loving relationships because, with conscious awareness, we can choose more optimal responses than our defensive habits. With repetition, these optimal responses can move up our primed hierarchies of conditioned responses until they become more automatic than our defenses.

You don't know me.

If your spouse looks at you with attraction/approval/yum, *and you don't believe they are really seeing you accurately,* you're likely to feel shame emotions at what feels like false high regard. These shame emotions can cue defensive impulses to avoid conscious awareness and lead to feeling emotionally separated by your spouse's lack of understanding. This dynamic happens frequently when someone who allows herself to normalize a diminished sense of self (has low self-worth) is praised and becomes uncomfortable instead of pleased. If I believe I have little value, I will be embarrassed by your positive regard.

On the other hand, if I refuse to acknowledge my own shadow aspects of immaturity and selfishness, I will not feel known by others because I don't feel deeply known by me. Individuals like Alice in the above example are often unaware of (and disinterested in) their shadow, which can result in life positions of pretending to be perfect and denying anything even vaguely unattractive or negative. This tends to create shallow relationships. If others point out Alice's shadow, she is likely to reject or attack them. A manipulative liar like Preston is a complementary spouse to Alice because he will either tell her what she wants to hear ("You're the best"), or be easily dismissed as a selfish liar when he says something unpleasant (after all, he *is* a selfish liar). Further, since she is not being self-reflective herself, Alice is unlikely to effectively advocate for Preston to be self-reflective about his shadow aspects, and thus is a complementary spouse for a man not wanting to look at his more immature attributes.

You *think* you know me.

On the other hand, not feeling known through *consciously* hiding aspects of self (as in hiding a secret affair), or experiencing your partner as *unable* to know you (as in Teresa despairing at John truly understanding her need for more romance), creates distance and reduces positive intimate charge. A common reaction of spouses consciously hiding an affair (or consciously hiding other important aspects of themselves) is to find their husband or wife boring. A huge aspect of being unfaithful is the constant knowledge that there is a shameful forbidden secret that has to always be guarded from discovery. The openness that affection and interest from a spouse generates can actually be irritating and threatening under these circumstances.

Believing your spouse is *unable* to know you tends to create both contempt and despair. During the dishes argument, Teresa felt contempt towards John for seeming to refuse to understand her need for more romantic engagement, and a sense of hopelessness at ever feeling romanced satisfactorily by him.

You know me and accept me.

If your spouse looks at you with attraction/approval/yum *and you subjectively experience them perceiving all of you,* you're likely to feel known and loved. Feeling known and loved is usually quite pleasurable and often involves impulses to respond in a complementary fashion by knowing and loving *all of your partner.* Rather than the common couple experience of conspiring to hide forbidden areas, you support each other in feeling and tolerating shadow (often involving shame emotions) and examining underlying internal representations. You feel safer doing this threatening activity with your own forbidden areas *because you subjectively feel that your partner knows and accepts all of you.* Teresa and John's last exchange in the therapy session constitute a peak third stage moment of this dynamic. Her "I love you baby. I know I can be a demanding bitch," and his, "Yeah, but you're my bitch, and when you demand love you deserve it," reflect the bliss of a couple feeling known and accepted by each other on all levels.

To the extent that you can maintain compassionate understanding and communicate your partner is known and loved, you are influencing your relationship towards greater intimacy. Couples where both partners consistently cultivate these qualities tend to have superior marriages. The way to influence your partner to do this is to practice doing it yourself.

Shame marital axiom #2: Accept your spouse, acknowledge feelings and impulses, and reach for love.

You might ask, "What if I'm feeling angry or critical towards my partner? How can I communicate attraction and acceptance then?" This brings us to shame marital axiom #2: Accept your spouse, acknowledge feelings and impulses, and reach for love. Consider the following two scenarios:

First version:

Wife: "You painted the room the wrong color."

Husband: "You gave me the damn paint!"

Wife: "Don't be angry."

Husband: *"She is so stupid. I'm stupid. I should have had her see the color on the wall before I started."* "I'm not angry!"

Second version:

Wife: "Don't be angry."

Husband: *"She is so stupid. I'm stupid. I should have had her see the color on the wall before I started. No, it is just a mistake. We'll paint it over."* "I am angry because I'm frustrated you don't like the color, and I did use the paint you gave me. Give me a minute to breathe and relax. We'll get the paint you want and do it right."

Which of these two men is more trustable to you? To me, it's a no-brainer. The second husband is taking responsibility for his feelings, acknowledging anger at his wife for cueing his feeling of failure for doing the job wrong (as in *"I'm stupid."*), and communicating care and respect. He is more trustable and attractive. You'll notice he is not attacking his wife for the impossible demand of "Don't be angry." An egalitarian second-stage husband might focus on this and lead the couple into a laborious processing session like the one John and Teresa had about her boredom. If successful, such processing would provide safety for their feelings (a good thing) and make some progress on the issues of her impossible demands and his angry reactions (also a good thing). On the other hand, if both assume responsibility for safety, it liberates them to immediately accept each other, acknowledge frustration, anger, and shame, and reach for love without the need for painful processing (a *really* good thing).

Dissociation and disidentification.

In the first version, the frustrated husband insisted he wasn't angry. In many cases this is the literal truth because people are often not consciously aware of what they are experiencing. This is dissociation where our brain cuts us off from a feeling, thought or impulse. Dissociation is a common defensive strategy that humans can naturally develop (especially as infants and toddlers) when they exceed their window of tolerance for overwhelming experiences such as terror, rage, or extreme shame.[4]

Disidentification involves *experiencing* painful feelings and thoughts while *not getting lost* in them. In the second version, the husband felt and acknowledged his anger and shame but did not let his amplified emotion (rage) or distorted perspectives (*"She is so stupid. I am stupid."*) dominate his consciousness. He experienced the feeling and was aware his emotion was amplified and his thought was distorted as he reached for more compassionate understanding (*"It is just a mistake. We'll paint it over."*). Integrating painful and/or forbidden thoughts and feelings usually requires feeling and acknowledging them and reaching for more compassionate perspectives and caring actions. Where dissociation tends to keep defensive structures in place, disidentification supports resolving defensives and integrating into more complex and mature states of healthy response.

Shame and the levels of erotic development.

The lover role in marriage is usually shared only with our spouse. In many cases, all lover relationships we engage in throughout life culminate in a marriage where fidelity is assumed (and statistically likely since married partners are generally faithful). For better or worse, marriage creates a partnership where a couple will sexually grow or sexually stagnate together.

David Deida suggests that there are six include and transcend levels of sexual development that begin with DNA using all life to reproduce itself, and end in the union of pure love and deepest consciousness. I'll briefly describe them:

- We're born to the **genetic level of sexuality** where the purpose of sex is to pass on our genes.

- We develop consciousness where we discover our bodies and want sex for pleasure. This is the **physiological level of sexuality**.

- As children age, they increasingly hunger to be included in family and tribal groups within which they want their sexuality to be considered *normal*. This is the **social level of sexuality** where the goal is acceptance.

- Teens and young adults increasingly crave intimate lover relationships where they yearn for fulfillment. This is the **psycho-emotional level of sexuality**.

- We can choose to consciously use erotic polarity to conduct energy through sexual bliss in service of healing and health. This is the **yogic level of sexuality**.

- Ultimately we can give our deepest gifts of consciousness and love to the universe through masculine presence opening feminine erotic radiance expressed through pleasure in the body. This is the **spiritual level of sexuality**.[5]

The purely genetic level of sexuality is instinctual, egocentric and free of conscious evaluation (though looks of disapproval can evoke physiological shame reactions starting at about one year old). Succeeding levels of sexuality involve more self-awareness and connection to (and care for) others. Our needs for approval from others and ourselves tend to shift in response to our emergent worldviews and goals of the moment. The subjective experience of shame can occur on all these levels and can help or hurt development, depending on temperament, personality, family system, gender roles, and processing skills.

Sexual shame begins at the physiological level when a child is disapproved of for displaying body parts, bodily functions, or engaging in pleasurable erotic activity like masturbation or looking/touching games with other children. The social conformist level of sexuality teaches children what thoughts, feelings, and practices are unacceptable, and shames them for engaging in such activities. In the emotional level, we can be ashamed of our own or our partner's lack of fulfillment. At the yogic level of sexuality we can feel shame for egocentric activity and subtle disapproval for sexuality that is not graceful or "spiritual."

At the spiritual level of sexuality, shame can be embraced wholeheartedly as a guide to deeper bliss and wider opening to pure Spirit. Authentic unity with all is acceptance of everything known and unknown, including all light and shadow. Wherever there is shame, there is a charged interface between an internal representation of how we or others should be (a should pattern) at odds with how we currently experience ourselves or others. In an atmosphere of total acceptance and commitment to spirit, we can use this charge to refine our should-patterns and/or our behaviors and integrate into more complex harmonies that empower us to give more, and thus open to deeper ecstasy, guided solely by what creates the most love and pleasure.

Shame marital axiom #3: Couples that consciously cultivate sexual pleasure and growth in themselves and their partners tend to be healthier and happier.

In the sexual journey everyone makes, lovers will often be our richest resources and/or our most profound blocks. This is especially true for husbands and wives. If you can courageously accept and explore your eroticism while accepting and supporting your spouse's, every aspect of marriage is enhanced. This is the yogic level of sexuality, which involves consciously pursing love, health, and healing through sexuality. Any time an individual or couple indulges impulses to avoid perceiving and integrating shameful sexual material, they are wasting a growth opportunity. Any time an individual or couple directs conscious attention towards sexual growth, they are practicing a yoga which leads to more moments of third stage erotic bliss, and supports marital health.

1. Witt (2005)

2. Schore (2003), Cozolino (2002)

3. Siegal (2005)

4. van der Kolk (2006)

5. Deida (2004)

11

Shame and Culture

From *All Good People*

Macy had an acid tongue
It's true, man, she could slash and cut
Howard's skin was laced with scars
He'd let it all go way too far

Howard hated what Macy did
"He's a pig," so she said
Just breathe and see it through
Good people can see it through

Just remember we're all good people
All good people, all good people
Don't you know that we're all good people
All good people, all good people

In November of 2006 Rupert Murdoch's News Corp. announced that it was canceling the publication of O.J. Simpson's book, *If I Did It,* and declining to screen Judith Regan's two-part TV interview with him supporting the book. This decision was completely based on public disgust and outcry at helping a convicted killer (he was found guilty in the civil trial) profit from the brutal murder of his ex-wife and her lover. Said Murdock, "I and senior management agree with the American public that this was an ill-considered project."[1] The L.A. Times article reporting the cancellation continued with, "News Corp. executives said that protests had reached a tipping point, with opposition coming from all quarters: the victims' families, viewers, station affiliates, advertisers, booksellers and even executives within the company."[2] Weeks later, Judith Regan, the originator of the project, was fired by Jane Friedman, HarperCollins' president and chief executive.[3] It's possible that the decisions to quash the project and fire Regan were driven to some extent by profit motives of broadcasters worried about consumer backlash, though arguably the project might have generated enormous revenues. Judith Regan had a twelve-year history of incredible success, largely from sensational celebrity biographies and right and left wing rants from TV and radio pundits. Apparently the major force in the decision to back off was the collective disgust, disapproval, and shame generated in response to the book and program. During the uproar, newscasts, newspapers and magazines were filled with variants of the question, "Have they no shame?"

Here is a therapy session with Teresa, John, Aaron, and Arial during Winter break after Aaron's first quarter at University of California at San Diego. Aaron is nineteen and Arial is sixteen:

Dr. Brown: "What do you all want to talk about today."

Teresa: "I want to talk about Aaron's behavior. Every since he left for college, he's been a jerk."

Aaron: "You're so full of it. I'm just growing up. You want me to stay your baby."

John: "You didn't used to say things like, 'You're full of it.'" (Aaron looks down.)

Arial: "Yeah, and you were mean to my friends when they came over to sew cheerleading outfits."

Aaron: "Cheerleading is so high school."

Arial: "Well *duh,* we're *in* high school."

Dr. Brown: "Aaron, what's it like in the dorms?"

Aaron: "I've talked about it. All my roommate Zack can talk about is screwing chicks and kicking ass. He thinks I'm a wimp for not cheating on tests. The other guys are fine, but I can't believe how much they drink and smoke pot, and they're always jamming each other; you know teasing and challenging."

Dr. Brown: "Sounds different from home." (Everyone laughs.)

Aaron: "It's not like I prefer it. The dorms are a different world."

Dr. Brown: "You're getting pushed by all this young, unsupervised male energy, and you have to push back."

Aaron: "Exactly. My family doesn't get it. If you're nice or honest, or don't want to get loaded, or don't want to do anything to get girls to have sex, the other guys think you're weak."

John: "You know better than that. I admire your values, and I'm glad you're not like Zack."

Teresa: "We didn't send you to college to learn to be rude."

Aaron: "I can see it when you talk about it. I'm sorry."

Dr. Brown: "Cultures we are embedded in influence us to conform to their values. We want to be accepted, and don't want to be viewed with disapproval or contempt. If we vary too much from a culture's values, the members' disapproval and expectations pull us towards conformity. Your family culture has values of caring for housemates and being considerate. Your dorm has values of being tough, not being sensitive, and being more egocentric and thrill-seeking. Your dorm culture pulls you away from your family standards about being considerate by viewing caring behavior as wimpy or shameful. Your family culture pulls you away from dorm standards of being a thick-skinned tough guy by viewing egocentric tough guy behavior as selfish and offensive."

Aaron: "So either way I'm screwed." (More laughter.)

Dr. Brown: "To the contrary. Paying attention to what *you* believe is right and discerning what your current culture's standards are cultivates the depth of consciousness to fit in anywhere while still being true to your developing values. Values are not static. Every time you feel guilty, embarrassed, or ashamed, and then compassionately self-reflect, you are refining your values. Any time someone presents you with a new perspective that attracts you in some way, you are refining your values. One of the reasons you go away to college is to have experiences like this that expand your worldview and challenge you to grow."

Aaron: "Most of the guys in my dorm just want to have fun and pass their classes. They could care less about expanding worldviews."

Dr. Brown: "And yet it's still happening with them, but not as consciously as with you. Research shows that the college experience tends to help broaden perspectives and increase success, so eventually most of your roommates will probably become more mature and responsible.[4] The problems you're having are partly a consequence of growing up in a self-reflective, considerate family which pulls you to be self-reflecting and considerate and reacts with distress when you're not."

Aaron: "I don't feel so bad for being such a macho jerk now. I guess I can learn how to adjust to dorm culture without getting drunk and cheating on tests."

Teresa: "I can't believe we're paying twenty-five thousand dollars a year so Aaron can be coerced to drink, use drugs, cheat on tests, learn how to be promiscuous, and be selfish." (Aaron rolls his eyes and begins a contemptuous response, but John heads him off.)

John: "Come on Teresa, remember what we were like in college?" (Teresa blushes, and John smiles fondly.) "There you go Aaron. Your mom would have given Zack a run for his money."

Teresa: "John!" (To laughter from the rest of the family.)

What drives us socially? What are the forces that motivate humans to establish societies and maintain social norms? Abraham Maslow suggested that needs for food, shelter, security, contact, and recognition dominate the first stages an individual's development. He called these "deficiency needs" because they each involved a sense of lack that needed to be addressed. As someone developed security in these areas (confidence that there would always be enough food, shelter, safety, contact, and recognition), they tended to start having needs to serve others, serve the world and deepen their own compassion and consciousness. Maslow called these "being needs" because there was a hunger to grow and give from a sense of fullness.[5] Freud thought that drives to create and destroy (Eros and Thanatos) were central to human society.[6] Victor Frankl taught that existential needs for meaning were primary in human development, and later researchers such as Robert Kegan have asserted that the instinct to create meaning is one of the main engines driving human development.[7] Alfred Adler thought the will to have power was the organizing principle of society.[8] Research has demonstrated merit in all of these conceptualizations.

Humans are genetically driven to relate, seek position on social hierarchies, create meaning, and be true to their masculine/feminine aspects/essences.

I believe that each human is driven to survive, relate, seek position on personally important social hierarchies[9], create meaning out of experience, and be true to their deepest masculine and/or feminine aspects and essence. These are genetic imperatives expressed at every level of development through our biochemistry (and especially our neurochemistry), through what draws our attention, through the emotions that saturate all experience, through the impulses we have, through our relating with others, and through the relative facility with which we process our feelings, thoughts, yearnings, and memories to support health and growth rather than sickness and stagnation.[10]

Humans are social beings. All of the needs and drives listed above are social to some extent. What are the internal forces that guide us to satisfy them more or less cooperatively within the cultures we're embedded in? Hunger for approval and avoidance of disapproval are the 600 pound gorillas of motivating forces towards social cohesion. Pain and pleasure, anger and fear, profit and loss, and impulses to attack and/or flee from threat are all significant influences on how people relate. None of these is more powerful in influencing us to comply with social norms than our hunger for social approval and our antipathy to the shame emotions cued by disapproval.

These principles are all reflected in the O.J. story and John and Teresa's family therapy session. Judith Regan (who began her literary career working for the *National Inquirer*) had great success mining the charged boundary between the culturally acceptable and culturally forbidden. As we explored in Chapter Seven, this interface is exciting and attractive if it does not elicit *too much* painful emotion. Judith Regan pushed this boundary too far and elicited a cultural upwelling of embarrassment, shame, and then rage directed at her and her company. In my opinion, Rupert Murdock and News Corp, following in the footsteps of governments, corporations, CEO's, and human organizations throughout history, avoided its shame by finding a scapegoat to take the heat. Regan (previously a corporate hero, generating fortunes for News Corp. by plunging into taboo areas) was now offered up as a human sacrifice to assuage the distress of the culture. Recognition and disapproval, shame and pride, acceptance in the group, or rejection by the group are all variations of the basic motivating forces that shape human needs to relate with others, establish and maintain position on personally important social hierarchies, create meaning out of experience, and be true to masculine/feminine aspects and essence.

The therapy session illustrates how culture both pulls us up to cultural standards, and holds us down when we begin to become different. Aaron was raised in an egalitarian, pluralistic environment within his family that was non-hierarchical, multi-cultural, and simultaneously espoused embracing multiple perspectives while being unconsciously contemptuous of differing viewpoints. Plunged into the egocentric, competitive, emotionally dog-eat-dog environment of the dorms, he was at first contemptuous of his roommates' apparent selfishness, but eventually succumbed to their contempt (and his desire for acceptance) enough to take on some of their values and behaviors. When he came home on break, his family was irritated and repulsed by his new perspectives and behaviors, thus pulling him back towards his old values. With Theo's help, the family began to consider the validity in both cultures, which influenced them to be more aware of their own reflexive contempt for differing worldviews. When Teresa was reminded by John that she once embraced a similar college worldview, she was first embarrassed, but then awakened a little (as reflected in her laughter) to a broader perspective. Culture pulls us up, but then holds us down *unless* we have the depth of consciousness to notice the interior and external forces influencing us, the wisdom to tolerate and explore distressing emotions, and the compassion and resolve to keep adjusting towards what feels like the highest good.

In the above examples, the "Have you no shame?" cultural responses to taboo violations demonstrate how collective approval and disapproval drive our shared moral values and influence our beliefs and behaviors. Complicating these processes are the cultural forces influencing us to deny or otherwise avoid feeling, acknowledging, and effectively processing shame emotions.

The elephant in the living room: hiding shame is often considered beautiful and moral.

Public sporting events are great windows on a culture's attitudes towards success and failure. In the United States, gifted athletes engage in difficult, dangerous competitions involving decades of rigorous training and subjectively enormous consequences, in front of thousands of often disinhibited spectators. Noise, crowding, anonymity, low lights, and intoxication are all disinhibiting forces[11] that can result in huge collective expressions of spontaneous approbation and/or disapprobation from crowds, depending upon the performance of the athletes. Any experienced competitor will tell you that cheers can turn into boos in seconds.

A successful athlete and his team will often celebrate good play with facial and bodily expressions of triumph like end zone dances, high fives, screams, and fist pumps. Home crowds generally love these victory displays, and cheer along with their heroes. When an opponent triumphs the result is more often silence than boos. There is a collective understanding that you do not boo success. On the other hand, if someone makes a mistake, or if an unpopular opponent steps on the field, the air can ring with boos, taunts, insults, and demeaning expressions of all kinds.

Celebrating success and behaving with apparent detachment when successful are usually welcomed by spectators and other competitors. Demonstrating shame at failure is despised by all. A player that hangs his head in shame after costly errors is often criticized by commentators, confronted by teammates, and booed by fans. In post-game interviews, it is considered attractive and moral for athletes to acknowledge errors and take responsibility. These are culturally acceptable responses to failure. Rarely do athletes report shame at crucial mistakes. The standard on and off the field, court, ring, or floor is to not show weakness and to never acknowledge shame. It is considered beautiful and good to acknowledge mistakes, but not to feel ashamed of them.

Taking responsibility for one's actions is considered a mark of maturity and mental health.[12] Tolerating the demeaning boos of thousands (or tens of thousands, or millions) with equanimity is admirable. These standards reflect the reality that standing unrecoiling and present in the face of humiliation is attractive and, *if authentic,* often signs of mature consciousness, especially to the competitive masculine in both men and women.[13] The healthy form of this is disidentification as in "I feel shame, but I am not shame because I am doing my best to take responsibility and do right." This is "Keeping your head up," which obviously refers to refusing to surrender to the universal phenomenon of looking down (due to sudden loss of muscle tone in shoulder, neck, and face muscles) in shame. The unhealthy form of standing unrecoiling is dissociation or outright lying, where an individual pretends to not feel a shame emotion, or is so lost in dissociation or narcissistic pathology that he or she actually feels no shame in the face of disapproval for mistakes, failure, powerlessness, or creating suffering for others. What does this tell us about shame and our culture?

Many cultures (including most of the U.S.) condition their members to selectively not see the elephant in the living room. All humans are socialized into standards of acceptable and unacceptable emotional responses, with shame often unacceptable.[14] Our individual defenses (which are largely biochemically driven tendencies to avoid experiences that originally couldn't be otherwise self-regulated) can become generalized into cultural standards of denial and other avoidance strategies that inform and reinforce parental messages to infants and toddlers. These children grow into adults who reinforce avoidance strategies in their children and so on through the ages. Nowhere is this so overwhelmingly obvious and colossally ignored than with the shame emotions. Individual shadow and cultural shadow are partly held in place, pushed where they are hard to perceive, by our reflexive avoidance of shame emotions.

Let's put the elephant to work

What if children and preschoolers (who *cannot* hold opposing concepts simultaneously) were taught to identify and acknowledge shame, *accept the feeling and themselves,* look for the rule they believe they're violating, and then either change their behavior to conform with the rule, or discuss the rule with a wise caregiver? This is well within the capacities of most elementary school brains. What if teenagers (who *can* hold opposing concepts like accepting yourself completely in the moment, while committing to a lifetime of change and growth) were taught to identify and acknowledge shame, accept the feeling and themselves, and evaluate their behavior and the underlying internal representations with the goal of constantly refining both to keep reaching for the highest good? What if they were further taught that *the harder this process was, the more deeply entrenched their shame avoidance systems probably were,* with corresponding needs for more support and exploration? The results of systematically including these skills in education would be a culture where the standard was to see and discuss the elephant in the living room, and use it's power and beauty to serve love.

1. Miller (2006)

2. Ibid

3. Getlin (2006)

4. Robins (2001)

5. Maslow (1962)

6. Freud (1961)

7. Frankl (2004), Kegan (1982)

8. Adler (1927)

9. Baker (2007)

10. Witt (2005)

11. www.aic.gov.au/publications/rrp/35/intro.pdf (2006).

12. Masterson (1981)

13. Deida (1997)

14. Wilber (2006)

12

Integration

From *Days of Joy*

Rock on man, play that funky song again
When Dylan sang, *Forever Young*
Add some drums, maybe boost it up a bit
Have some wine my friend

These are days that might not come again
These are days of joy
These are days that we can share as friends
These are days of joy

These are days of joy
Sun cascading down
We will keep the old songs alive
In the winter time

Aaron graduated from college with honors, got his real estate license, and began working with a local developer in Santa Barbara. At twenty-four he met Joanna who worked for a high tech firm that had a contract with Homeland Security to design and build sensors that could detect radioactive material. They instantly were attracted and quickly became lovers. The following is an individual therapy session with Dr. Theo Brown that Aaron scheduled after he and Joanna had their first big fight:

Dr. Brown: "It's good to see you Aaron. What's up?"

Aaron: "I met this great woman, Joanna, and we've been dating for five months now."

Dr. Brown: "I'm happy for you."

Aaron: "Yeah, well we just had this huge fight. I don't know what happened. We were driving to her parents for Thanksgiving and she just went off on me."

Dr. Brown: "She just went off on you."

Aaron: "All I said was I was looking forward to meeting her parents, and she told me to stop being sarcastic. I told her I wasn't being sarcastic, and that I really was looking forward to it, and she called me liar. I got offended and it got worse from there."

Dr. Brown: "How did it end?"

Aaron: "We argued all the way to L.A. Finally she admitted that sometimes her Mom's drinking embarrasses her on holidays. She also said we've only been lovers since August and our relationship is a big deal to her and feels kind of new and delicate. I told her it was a big deal to me too, and that I wouldn't blame her for anything her parents did. We felt better by the time we arrived. It all worked out fine. They were nice people and nobody got drunk at Thanksgiving, but Joanna has never acted that way before."

Dr. Brown: "What way?"

Aaron: "Mean and sarcastic. It was like she was a different person."

Dr. Brown: "What was your part of the fight? How did you get hooked into a long painful argument?"

Aaron: "What do you mean? I had no choice. She was saying nasty things and acting all suspicious, like I was being mean and lying to her."

Dr. Brown: "What was valid about that?"

Aaron: (Blushing and looking away.) "I wasn't very nice after she called me a liar. I said a few things."

Dr. Brown: "You're usually a pretty mellow guy. You have to feel really injured to get nasty."

Aaron: "I just can't stand being treated like dirt. I don't know why stuff like that still gets to me. I accept who I am. I know I'm not perfect."

Dr. Brown: "No, really?"

Aaron: (Laughing.) "Come on. Seriously. All that work I did in college and in therapy. I do accept myself. Why do I get so outraged when someone I love gets down on me?"

Dr. Brown: "You talk as if accepting yourself is something that you do, and then that's the end of it."

Aaron: "Isn't that the way it works? Isn't that what Carl Rogers said? You face who you are and have unconditional positive regard; you know, total acceptance."

Dr. Brown: (*"He's only twenty-four and knows so much."*) "You've got it partly right. Who do you know that has total acceptance for themselves or anyone else?"

Aaron: "I don't know. My parents do, mostly. You do." (This surprises Theo enough so that he starts choking on the tea he was drinking while Aaron was talking.) "What? You've always been there for my family. You never seem to be mean or paranoid or whatever."

Dr. Brown: (*"Where to start?"*) "First of all, thank-you for your confidence. You're right I have been there for your family. My point is that self-acceptance or acceptance of others isn't something you do and that's it. It's a process or a skill that you hone your entire lifetime. There's not a day that goes by where I don't catch myself being contemptuous of somebody else, or ashamed of myself. I can't read the paper without getting angry at somebody causing unnecessary suffering, or miss some minor thing at work without feeling guilty. I've learned to notice non-acceptance, self-reflect on what's going on, find where I need to shift my behavior and perspectives and then move on."

Aaron: "Don't you ever get there? Do we feel ashamed and angry forever?"

Dr. Brown: "In my opinion, thinking you can be so evolved that you never get angry, frightened, or ashamed is one of the biggest mistakes many psychotherapy systems and spiritual traditions make. Because the originators and practitioners of these systems teach and write while feeling self-acceptance and unity, they unconsciously suggest that we can eventually somehow 'get there,' and never have to feel ashamed, distorted, mean or confused again. There is a subtle message that we will become pure caring and never selfish. I believe this is an elaboration of the shame avoidance defenses that all humans share. The reality is that the more we work on knowing and accepting ourselves, and the more we cultivate self-reflection (like the mind-fulness exercises I taught you when you were sixteen), the more moments of self-acceptance we have, and the more moments of unity we feel with every-thing. Over time we have progressively more of these moments. Hasn't that been the case for you the last seven years?" (Aaron nods.) "These moments of acceptance and unity can increase and flow together like pools, so we have them more routinely and get better at cultivating them. We never lose our human capacities for pleasure at positive recognition, and shame at disap-proval. We never lose our human reactions of anger, fear, anxiety, sadness, shame emotions, or selfishness. We will always, episodically, have our defenses cued and have to self-regulate or not, depending on our levels of knowledge and practice."

Aaron: "So, something Joanna said cued my defenses?" (Theo nods.) "It was when she called me a liar and got contemptuous. I hate that."

Dr. Brown: "At that moment, in your deepest heart, what was your impulse?"

Aaron: (He looks down.) "I wanted to slap her across the face. But I'd never *do* that."

Dr. Brown: "Of course not. But do you accept that sometimes you'll get mad and have that impulse?"

Aaron: "I guess." (Theo looks skeptical.) "OK. I think it's wrong to feel like hitting your lover. I don't want to be like that."

Dr. Brown: "Can you accept that you are like that? That you'll have feelings, thoughts, and impulses you're ashamed of for the rest of your life, and that each time you feel them your work will be to notice, accept, self-reflect and then do your best to choose compassionate perspectives and healthy actions?"

Aaron: "Isn't there an easier way?" (This gets both of them laughing.)

The integration-of-defenses line of development

We've already established how each of us can direct our own personal evolution on many developmental lines with increasing conscious awareness from birth to death. Since development is *include* and transcend, we never lose defensive reflexes or tendencies. What we *can* do is become more aware, honest, and effec-tive at using our defenses as opportunities to grow rather than as blocks to health and intimacy. I believe there is a developmental line for effectively exploring and integrating defenses into larger, wiser, more complex frameworks that support more caring, compassionate, and effective worldviews. I call it the integration-of-defenses line and (like most other developmental lines) progress on it requires development on a variety of other lines including:

- Cognitive development to conceptualize difficult constructs like, "Have a standard to do right and accept myself fully, while understanding that I'll always make mistakes and periodically feel ashamed."

- Moral development to become progressively more caring of wider groups of beings, while understanding there will always be more subtle nuances of ethical and moral decision making stretching ahead.

- Interpersonal development to be able to acknowledge, integrate, and appropriately self-regulate hunger for contact and approval, dependence on others, and disapproval from others.

- Psychosexual development to increasingly understand and be true to masculine/feminine aspects and essence.

The added elements of the integration-of-defenses line of development are the relative abilities to discern, feel, tolerate, and effectively process the amplified or numbed emotions, distorted perspectives, and destructive impulses present in all defenses. This is further combined with the relative abilities to cultivate empathy and self-reflection while in defensive states. Development on this line can be observed from a number of perspectives such as:

- Expanding abilities to productively process critical feedback of all kinds.

- Increasingly subtle awareness of defensive cues.

- An increasing sense of personal responsibility to self-regulate defensive reactions.

- A decreasing frequency of allowing defensive states to blossom.

- Increasing ability to self-regulate to a state of healthy response *from any level* of defensive reaction.

Arguably, the integration-of-defenses line is a central feature of most shadow work, since what we don't see is often obscured by defensive states and much shadow is turning away from personal responsibility instead of embracing it. Some of the main obstacles to growth on the integration-of-defenses line are the unique combinations of reflexive avoidance reactions to shame emotions (and shadow material in general) that all of us develop as infants and children. An added difficulty in risking empathy and self-reflection in defensive states is that (like Aaron in his argument with Joanna) we'll often be called upon to practice these skills while feeling threatened, provoked, or disapproved of by others.

Here are Preston and Alice driving to The Paradise Café in Santa Barbara to have dinner with Aaron and Joanna. They've never met Joanna, partially because Aaron is somewhat embarrassed socially by his father and stepmother and has had progressively less to do with them since college. His dad brags and flirts with his friends and dates, and Alice's relentless self-absorption has always made Aaron uncomfortable. The way Preston and Alice deal with this is to fight about Aaron. Alice maintains that Aaron is "stuck up" and has been biased against her by Teresa's "bad-mouthing," while Preston denies any problems and assumes that Aaron and his friends find Alice and him delightful and attractive:

> Alice: (She's nervous and worried about being critically judged, so she instinctively looks for someone to attack.) "I hope this chick Aaron's with isn't as uptight as he is."

> Preston: (He's also unconsciously anxious about the dinner. Aaron hardly ever makes overtures for contact and, even though Preston denies it, he's always felt disapproved of by Aaron. Alice is now giving him an outlet for his stress.) "It's no big deal. Don't worry, you'll lighten up after your first margarita."

> Alice: "There you go, always taking his side against me."

> Preston: (He senses her on the edge of an explosion and feels a tingle of fear. Alice is capable of almost any level of embarrassing outrage when she's mad. He quickly tries to placate her.) "Come on honey. You know you're my number one girl."

> Alice: (Caustically.) "I am until your number two girl shows up, so fuck you."

> Preston: "Come on, we're here. Let's just go and have a good time. OK?" (Alice ignores him as she climbs out of the car.)

Preston and Alice are low on the integration-of-defenses line of development. Neither of them is conscious of (or curious about) their anxiety, shame, or defensive states. Both are allowing and fueling negative emotions, supporting distorted perspectives, and indulging destructive impulses. Neither is honestly self-reflecting or empathizing, other than Preston's codependent awareness that Alice is dangerously upset and he needs to placate her somehow. Empathy in service of fear and accommodation is codependent adaptation rather than caring.

Their integration-of-defenses immaturity is a natural function of decades of indulging rather than challenging defenses. Preston and Alice have practiced the same bad habits endlessly since infancy, resulting in reinforcing and deepening the neural networks they established as children to avoid shameful or otherwise unpleasant feelings, thoughts, and perspectives. As adults they've created complementary relationships with each other and others that support (rather than effectively challenge) these bad habits. When their defensive states have been evoked, they've consistently refused to take responsibility for them, and practiced avoiding (rather than feeling and examining) painful emotions and internal representations.

Across town, Teresa, John, and Arial (now twenty-two and a senior in college) are walking out of the movie *World Trade Center*. All three are distressed by the movie's violence and the 911 restimulations:

Arial: "I can't believe people would cause so much horror for nothing."

John: "They believed they were doing the right thing. We've killed thirty times that many innocent people in Iraq."

Arial: "Don't defend them! Look what they did to those poor people."

Teresa: "He's not defending them. He's just saying that it's more complicated."

Arial: "Let him speak for himself, Teresa. You don't know everything."

Teresa: (As the anger wells up in her she takes a deep breath. *"Come on. You feel the same way about zealot maniacs. We're all hungry and upset."*) "You're right. I shouldn't speak for other people, but we're all hungry and upset. Let's go out to eat and talk about it later."

Arial: (*"The whole thing really gets to me. I hate cruelty and now I'm being mean to Teresa. She doesn't deserve it."* Her face suddenly feels hot. *"You shouldn't go off on people Arial. I need to watch out when I'm upset."*) "I'm sorry I snapped. All that stupid suffering was hard to bear."

John: (*"I was defending them. Just because Iraq is a train wreck doesn't mean the terrorists were justified."*) "I agree it is completely despicable what they did. Sometimes I get so mad about the war that my thinking gets distorted. Teresa's right, let's get some dinner and talk more about it later."

Here are three people who are each deep on the integration-of-defenses line. As their defensive systems are cued, all three of them self-reflect on their amplified emotions and begin self-soothing. As distorted perspectives and destructive impulses constellate, they examine and change them while tolerating shame and anger and reaching out empathetically to each other. Even though it looks relatively simple, these abilities are the results of years of conscious effort on everybody's part.

Complexity theory tells us that open systems with differentiated parts that don't get lost in rigidity or chaos naturally move towards greater complexity *which often looks more simple.* Sitting in the car with John, Teresa, and Arial, an observer would feel that their conversation was reasonable, caring, and not that dramatic or negatively charged. *It would look simple.* Sitting in Preston and Alice's car would yield an entirely different experience. There is danger and emotional violence in the air, with a sense that unpleasant things might happen at any moment. *It would look complicated.* The more we practice making good decisions, the more routinely we self-regulate distressing emotions, perspectives and impulses into states of healthy response before they blossom into defensive states and patterns. Healthy states often look more simple than defensive states but actually reflect more depth, integration, and complexity.

Habits of healthy response free our consciousness to search for new levels of sophistication in dealing with ourselves and others. Preston and Alice will continue to keep getting caught in the same loops of avoiding awareness and responsibility for defensive states, which will keep resulting in internal and relational suffering enacted in the same patterns over numerous situations. John, Teresa, and Arial have cultivated internal representations of themselves as people who don't immediately attack when they're mad and who self-reflect when they feel ashamed. They've practiced these skills and perspectives enough that they notice the emotional and cognitive signals of violating a should-pattern and instinctively self-reflect instead of avoid. By doing this they grow incrementally each time they take responsibility for a defensive reaction, and gradually develop more complex and effective responses to distress. By consistent practice *they have moved self-reflection ahead of avoidance on their hierarchies of primed responses to shame.* Just as a professional tennis player's moves look more simple and elegant than a novice's, people deep on the integration-of-defenses line appear as if they are engaging in simple self-evident adjustments when dealing with defensive distortions. They make it look easy.

Just as a professional tennis player can set and accomplish goals a novice is incapable of, individuals deep on the integration-of-defensives line can move into levels of understanding, compassion, intimacy, and self-regulation that are unavailable to the less mature. At each step of the way, a major challenge is feeling, tolerating, and effectively processing shame emotions.

Why shame is a key to integration

In previous chapters we've explored consciousness as interior to countless internal relationships we have with ourselves in the present/past/future. These internal relationships naturally develop as our brains grow into the capacities for explicit memory and symbolic communication guided by interpersonal relationships with caregivers. Our internal relationships with various aspects of ourselves involve potentially infinite perspectives. Social relationships with others similarly involve potentially infinite perspectives. *Every internal or interpersonal relationship* has the capacity for approval or disapproval from another or ourselves in reality or fantasy. We crave interior and external approval, and are generally pleased when we feel it. We are distressed by interior and external disapproval, and often feel a shame emotion when we experience it. Infants and children can't effectively self-regulate shame emotions and so learn to avoid them, leading to the defensive avoidance strategies that inhibit growth on many developmental lines. Our integration-of-defenses line reflects our developing abilities to effectively confront and use avoidance strategies in service of love and growth. Increasing psychological health can be conceptualized as refinement of should-systems (internal representations), progressively more coherent autobiographical narratives, more integrated brains, more love and satisfaction in relationships, more mature self-awareness, and increasing depth on the integration-of-defenses line. Arrest on this line potentially blocks any of these aspects of psychological health.

From before birth, our brains absorb perceptual inputs and create internal representations (unconscious predictions) about how we, others, and things should be. As social beings, the moral aspects of these predictions (what is right and wrong) are guided culturally first by approval/disapproval from caregivers, and later include approval/disapproval from ourselves, others, and imagined others. Our brains constantly scan the environment and, when there are variations from how we predict things should be, they bring it to our attention. Often the way our brain brings to our attention that *we* are not being consistent with how *we* should be is with a shame emotion.

If we practice avoidance, we get better at avoiding. This leads to more strongly entrenched defenses, compromised intimacy, and diminished growth. If we feel, acknowledge, tolerate and self-reflect on the shame emotions, searching for truth, compassion, and caring, we tend to alter our behaviors to fit our internal-representation and/or refine our internal representations to reflect greater compassion and depth of consciousness. This leads to integration, enhanced intimacy, and growth. The more we practice, the better we get.

Shame as choke point

A choke point in a dynamic system is a place where a small block can create a major disruption.[1] The convergence of two highways is a choke point for the traffic pattern where an accident or roadblock can freeze a whole transportation network.

Since all humans learn early to avoid shame, and self-reflecting on shame emotions is an essential process for movement on many developmental lines, shame emotions are potential choke points. If we avoid feeling and processing, we create blocks that inhibit movement. If we feel and effectively process, we enhance movement and support ongoing transformation. Depth on the integration-of-defenses line reflects progressively more easily feeling, tolerating, and effectively self-reflecting on painful emotions, which results in regular refinement of should-patterns and behaviors towards truth, love, and compassion. This process inevitably leads us to deeper spirituality.

1. De Becker (1997)

13

Shame as Spiritual Guide

From *Wind of History*

The wind of history has come again today
The wind of history will blow us all away
The wind of history is rushing cross the line
Can never be denied

I stood with my face into the wind of history
Saw Thermopylae
Buddha teaching the present moment
Inquisition and Renaissance
Pure consciousness
Radiant love in the wind
In the present moment, ah …
In the present moment, ah …

Let's visit John and Teresa at sixty-two. It's been two years since the flirting episode with Jo, and life is good. John is just waking up on a clear Sunday morning in December. He looks down at Teresa sleeping beside him:

John: (*"She looks like a kid when she's asleep. O no! I almost forgot it's Arial's birthday next week. I need to get her a present."* Feeling relieved at remembering his daughter's birthday, he slowly sits up and looks at the mountains outside the bedroom window.)

Teresa: (She feels the motion, opens her eyes and smiles up at John. *"He still looks good. Who would have thought we'd be together in our sixties.)* "Good morning, baby. What's cooking, good looking?"

John: (As he bends down and kisses her he feels a flutter of desire followed by a spark of guilt. *"We haven't made love in a week. I've been too busy at work and haven't been paying enough attention."* He kisses her more intensely.) "You feel good."

Teresa: (*"He's always interested Sunday morning when he doesn't have work. I wish I was more important that work."* The irritation shifts into shame. *"Relax girl. At least he's interested. Open up to your man."* As she relaxes and embraces him, he becomes more intensely connected and she gets turned on.) "Come here you rascal." (They proceed to make exquisite morning love. After hanging out and talking for a while in bed, they eventually get up, shower, and start making breakfast.)

John: (Looking at the pine trees outside the kitchen window, he feels the power of nature surrounding them and remembers he hasn't meditated this weekend.) "I haven't meditated since Thursday."

Teresa: "Didn't you say last week you were going to meditate every day?"

John: (*"Who are you to talk? You hardly ever meditate. Lighten up John. She does yoga three days a week. Besides, women are turned off by men who don't follow through."*) "I think I will right now."

Teresa: (*"There I go being critical. We were having fun."*) "I'm sorry. I didn't mean to be the meditation police."

John: (He knows exactly what she's thinking.) "No, it's good you reminded me. When I say I'm going to do something, I want to do it. It will only take a half hour." (He walks into the other room and meditates facing out into the meadow behind their house. Teresa finishes making breakfast with a happy smile on her face.)

What is spirituality? Ken Wilber defines spirituality as a line of development, as a quality of experience, and as a characteristic of the upper levels of most developmental lines.[1] David Deida suggests that living the third stage is allowing yourself to be an unobstructed instrument of spirit in whatever ways are consistent with your deepest purpose, your sexual essence, and what most opens the moment.[2]

Many practitioners of contemplative spiritual traditions from all over the world describe similar experiences. They report a sense of unity with all beings, of remembering what has always been, or of waking up to an experience of fullness, emptiness, oneness, or all encompassing love that feels connected to everyone and available to everyone.[3] Some interpersonal neurobiologists believe that this experience is partly a restimulation of neural networks laid down in utero when we were literally one with the oceanic embrace of the womb, and our brains scanned and recorded the symbiotic experience of oneness in our implicit memories.[4] Interestingly, since such states of unity are generally blissful and characterized by wide, even universal, acceptance, there is little or no room in them for shame emotions. Certainly a non-dual experience of unity has little or no shame since disapproval/approval are dualistic constructs (some entity must approve/disapprove of something else). On the other hand, I doubt that any realizer throughout history (who has to inhabit a human body with human needs and relationships) has ever occupied a permanent state of non-dual awareness. I suspect that the quality of global acceptance in transcendent states has led to fallacious assumptions that spiritual growth or enlightenment means an end to shame emotions and defensive states, rather than extreme deepening on the integration-of-defenses line of development. Such depth does not banish shame emotions or defensive reactions but instead integrates them with everything else into complex systems of radical acceptance and compassion for all. The larger our acceptance, the less we privilege pleasure over pain, or caring impulses over destructive ones. Instead, we reach for truth, love, and growth in all experience and all internal representations.

We encounter the infinite early, and deal with it using the tools we have.

Socially and neurobiologically, I believe that there are forces other than implicit memories of the womb at work in transcendent states of unity. As we develop the capacities for symbolic communication, with knowledge of past, present, and future, we are confronted with infinite perspectives internally and interpersonally. Much has been made of each human's discovery of his or her own mortality, and childhood is full of fears of monsters, loss, death, and betrayal. But knowledge of our own death is just part of a staggering awakening process. If we contain infinite perspectives and can share infinite perspectives, then we somehow both contain and are part of the infinite. Conscious awareness arises out of the crucibles of potentially infinite internal and interpersonal relationships. Spiritual awakening often seems to involve a direct experience of this sense of both containing and being part of nature, emptiness, God, or all non-dual existence, and it often feels like something that we've always known that we're remembering or waking up to.

Children go through predictable stages of explaining the infinite. Toddlers (with pre-operational, non-rational cognitive abilities) have a magic orientation where they can subjectively experience themselves omnisciently manipulating the universe. School age children (with concrete either/or cognitive abilities) have a mythic orientation where they often attribute divine powers to parents, superheroes, or Gods. Teenagers (with formal operational cognitive abilities to inhabit "what if" scenarios and hold competing concepts simultaneously) can look for rational principles that explain spiritual phenomena. Mature adults (with post-formal operational cognitive abilities to integrate logic and intuition or post-post-formal operational cognitive abilities to have a felt participation in the subtle energetic forces that connect and influence everything) can inhabit stable states of oneness with all of nature or all of creation.

Much processing of the above happens in consciousness, which is quite likely interior to our infinite internal and interpersonal systems of relationships. *Each one* of those relationships has the capacity for approval and/or disapproval. As we've explored in depth, disapproval can evoke a shame emotion, which informs us that we are somehow not being consistent with our should-patterns. If felt, tolerated, examined, and effectively acted upon, shame emotions accelerate integration and development, and thus support both vertical and horizontal health. According to Ken Wilber, the higher the altitude on a given line of development, the stronger the sense of subjective spiritually.[5]

In the Sunday morning example with John and Teresa, shame emotions served as guides in a number of ways. After working on personal and relational development for many years, John and Teresa are deep on the integration-of-defenses line of development. They both feel the early irritation and shame signals that subtly inform them of constellating defensive states, and reflexively respond with awareness, self-reflection, and adjustment. It looks easy and, for them at this stage of their development, it often is easy. The paths they had to walk to get to this point were not easy at all, and their apparently effortless intimacy reflects decades of hard work and incredible internal sophistication.

All of their distressed moments were seeds of defensive states, cued mainly by shame emotions, that were translated into love and growth by two people who had paid the dues of struggling to develop and do right throughout their lives. Any one of these seeds, if allowed to sprout into a defensive state, could have ruined the morning, the day, or the week. If either John or Teresa had indulged one of these states, it would have pressured the other to respond with complementary pathology. Instead, they used the subtle beginnings of defenses as guides to love, and supported each other synergistically in the process; a form of shared spiritual practice.

John noticed his parental guilt at not remembering Arial's birthday, focused on getting her a card and present, and moved on. Similarly, he felt sexual shame of not initiating sex in a week, had the insight that he'd let himself be too distracted by work, and made an overture. Teresa was ashamed of her irritation, and relaxed into pleasurable connection without indulging the angry distorted perspective that John's work was more important to him than her. John felt masculine shame at not following through on his meditation commitment that was complemented by Teresa's feminine shame for possibly injuring love with her reminder. He resisted attacking her and she resisted attacking herself while trusting him to not blame her.

John's personal myth is that he is the hero who is committed to deep soul's purpose and serving the ones he loves. Teresa's personal myth is that she has gradually opened her heart to be independent, dependent, in charge, or surrendering to love's demands as a full spectrum woman. Both of these stories constitute coherent autobiographical narratives. John and Teresa's decisions and responses reflect depth on cognitive, interpersonal, psychosexual, moral, spiritual, and integration-of-defenses lines of development.

David Deida is a spiritual teacher who advocates extending spiritual practice beyond church, temple, or meditation cushion to everyday life. He maintains that strong spiritual practice is feeling life's vicissitudes, challenges, and demands, and loving through them while giving your best gifts.[6] This is often hardest when feeling shame emotions but, if we can learn to identify them, tolerate them, self-reflect on them, and adjust our internal representations and actions in service of compassion and truth, the shame emotions can be among our best spiritual guides.

1. Wilber (2006), (2004)

2. Deida (2003)

3. Almaas (2002), Wilber (2006)

4. Siegal (2005)

5. Wilber (2006)

6. Deida (2003)

References

Adler, Alfred. (1927). *The Practice and Theory of Individual Psychology.* International Library of Psychology

Alexander, Charles N., and Langer, Ellen J. (1990). *Higher Stages of Human Development, Perspectives on Adult Growth.* New York: Oxford University Press

Almaas, A. H., (2002). *Facets of Unity, The Enneagram of Holy Ideas.* Boston: Shambala

Baker, Sherry. (2007). *The Home Team Advantage ... and Other Sex Hormone Secrets.* Psychology today, (Jan./Feb. 2007).

Bandura, Albert. (1973). *Aggression: a Social Learning Analysis.* Prentice-Hall

Barratt, Barnaby. (2005). *Sexual Health and Erotic Freedom.* Philadelphia: Xlibris

Baumeister, R. F. and Leary M. R. (1995). *Desire For Interpersonal Attachments as a fundamental human motivation.* Psychological Bulletin, 11. 7. 497–529

Beck, Don Edward, and Cowan, Christopher C. (1996). *Spiral Dynamics; mastering values, leadership, and change.* Malden, MA: Blackwell Publishing

Bjerklie, David. (December 4, 2006). *Laughter.* Time Magazine. New York: Time Inc.

Blum, Deborah. (2002). *Love at Goon Park.* Perseus Publishing

Bowlby, J. (1988). *A secure base: Parent-child attachment and healthy human development.* New York: Basic Books

Bowen, M. (1961). *Family Psychotherapy.* American Journal of Orthopsychiatry. 31: 40–60

Bradshaw, John. (1990). *Homecoming, Reclaiming and Championing Your Inner Child.* New York: Bantam Books

—————-. (1988) *On the Family, a Revolutionary Way of Self-Discovery.* Deerfield Beach, Florida: Health Communications, Inc.

Brizendine, Louann. (2006). *The Female Brain.* New York: Morgan Road Books

Buss, D. M. (1999). *Evolutionary Psychology: The New Science of Mind.* Boston, MA: Allyn and Bacon

Campbell, Joseph. (1949) *The Hero With a Thousand Faces.* Princeton: Princeton University Press.

Carnes, Patric. (2002). *Out of the Shadows, Understanding Sexual Addiction.* Hazelden, Minn.

Carr, Jimmy and Greeves, Lucy. (2006). *Only Joking, What's so Funny About Making People Laugh?* New York: Gotham Books.

Cassidy, J., & Shaver, P. (Eds.). (1999), *Handbook of attachment: Theory, research, and clinical applications.* New York: Guilford Press.

Cloniger, Robert C. (2004). *Feeling Good, the Science of Well-Being.* Oxford University Press

Cozolino, Louis J. (2002). *The Neuroscience of Psychotherapy.* New York: W.W. Norton & Co.

Crepeau, Margaret (1992). *Fears about Tears? Why crying is good for you.* Vibrant Life Nov.–Dec.

Darwin, Charles. (1872). *The Expression of Emotions in Man and Animals.* London: John Murray

De Becker, Gavin. (1997). *The Gift of Fear, and other survival signals that protect us from violence.* New York: Dell Publishing

Debroski, T. M., MacDougal J. M., (1985). *Components of Type A, hostility, and anger-in: relationship to angiographic findings.* Psychosomatic Medicine. Volume 47, Issue 3

Dee, Thomas S. (2005). *Teachers and the Gender Gaps in Student Achievement.* NBER Working Paper No. W11660, September, 2005

Deida, David. (2004). *Enlightened Sex.* Boulder, Colorado: Sounds True (audio recording)

—————-. (1995). *Intimate Communion.* Deerfield Beach: Health Communications, Inc.

—————-. (1997). *The Way of the Superior Man.* Austin: Plexus

—————-. (2006). *David Deida, live, volumes 1, 2, 3.*

Dement, William C. and Vaughan, Christopher. (1999). *The Promise of Sleep.* New York: Dell

Diagnostic and Statistical Manual of Mental Disorders 4th edition: Washington D.C. American Psychiatric Association

Dobson, Louise. (2006). *What's your humor style?* Psychology Today, July, 2006.

Druck, Andrew. (1989). *Four Therapeutic Approaches to the Borderline Patient.* Northvale, New Jersey: Jason Aronson Inc.

Enard, Wolfgang, and Paabo, Svante. (2004). *Comparative Primate Genomics.* Annu. Rev. Genomics Hum. Genet. 5:351–78

Feller, Ben. (2006). *Teacher's Gender.* Santa Barbara News Press, November, 2006

Fisher, Helen. (2004). *Why We Love: the Nature and Chemistry of Romantic Love.* New York: Henry Holt

Frankl, Viktor. (2004). *Man's Search for Meaning. An Introduction to Logotherapy.* Boston: Beacon and Random House, first published 1946

Freud, Sigmund. (1961) *Civilization and its Discontents.* New York: Notion

Freud, Sigmund. (1949). *An Outline of Psycho-Analysis.* New York: W.W. Norton and Company.

Gelb, Michael J. (1988). *Present Yourself!* Torrance, Ca: Jalmar Press

Getlin, Josh. (December 16, 2006). *Publisher Fired After Furor Over O.J. Simpson.* Los Angeles Times

Gilbert, Daniel. (2006). *Does Fatherhood Make You Happy?* New York: Time Magazine, June 19.

Gibson, Lydalyle. (2006). *Mirrored Emotion.* Chicago: University of Chicago Magazine, April, 2006

Gilbert, P. (1995). *Biopsychosocial approaches to evolutionary theory as aids to integration in clinical psychology and psychotherapy.* Clinical Psychology and Psychotherapy. 2. 135–156

Gilbert, P. and Miles, J. (eds). (2002). *Body Shame, Conceptualization, Research and Treatment.* New York: Brunner-Routledge, Taylor and Francis Group

Gilligan, Carol. (1993). *In a Different Voice: Psychological Theory and Women's Development.* Cambridge, Mass.: Harvard University Press

Gilliland, B. E., & James, R. K. (1998). *Theories and strategies in counseling and psychotherapy.* Boston: Allyn & Bacon

Giordano, Suzy. (2006). *Twelve Hours' Sleep by Twelve Weeks Old, a Step-by-Step Plan for Baby Sleep Success.* New York: Dutton

Gottman, John. (2005). Presented at a conference, *The Anatomy of Intimacy.* Foundation for the Contemporary Family, UC Irvine, November 5 and 6.

—————, (2001). *The Relationship Cure, a 5 Step Guide for Building Better Connections with Family, Friends, and Lovers.* New York: Crown Publishing

Hawkins, Jeff. (2000). *On Intelligence.* New York: Henry Holt and Company

Hayes, S.C., Strosahl, K., and Wilson, K. G. (1999). *Acceptance and Commitment Therapy: An Experimental Approach to Behavior Change.* New York: Guilford Press

Hebb, Donald. (1949). *The organization of behavior: A neuropsychological theory.* New York: Wiley

Hutson, Matthew. (2006). *The heat of the moment: what will you do when in the mood?* Psychology Today, September 1, 2006

Johnson, Susan. (2005). Presented at a conference, *The Anatomy of Intimacy.* Foundation for the Contemporary Family, UC Irvine, November 5 and 6.

Jung, Carl G. (1961) *Memories, Dreams, and Reflections.* New York: Random House

————, (1959). *The Archetypes and the Collective Unconscious.* Princeton: Princeton University Press

————, (1959). *The Basic Writings of C. G. Jung,* ed. Violet Staub, De Laszlo, New York: The Modern Library

Kabat-Zinn, Jon. (2005). *Coming to Our Senses; healing ourselves and the world through mindfulness.* New York: Hyperion

Kahneman, Daniel. (1999). *Well-Being: Foundations of Hedonic Psychology.* Portland, Oregon: Book News, Inc.

Kaufman, Gershen. (1980). *Shame, The Power of Caring.* Rochester, Vermont: Schenkman Books, Inc.

Kegan, Robert. (1982) *The Evolving Self: Problems and Process in Human Development.* Cambridge, Mass: Harvard University Press

Kernberg, Otto. (1975). *Borderline Conditions and Pathological Narcissism.* Northvale, New Jersey: Jason Aronson Inc.

Kinsey, Alfred Charles. (1948). *Sexual Behavior in the Human Male.* Indiana University Press

————, (1953). *Sexual Behavior in the Human Female.* Indiana University Press

Leary, M. R. (1995) *Self-esteem as an interpersonal monitor: The sociometer hypothesis.* Journal of Personality and Social Psychology. 68. 519–530

Lemonick, Michael D. (2004). *The Chemistry of Desire.* New York: Time Magazine, Jan. 19, 2004.

————. Dorfman, Andrea. (2006). *What makes us different?* New York: Time Magazine, October 9

————. (2005). *The Bully Blight.* New York: Time Magazine, April 18

Levine, Judith. (2002). *Harmful to Minors.* Minneapolis: University of Mineapolis Press

Liedloff, Jean. *The Continuum Concept.* Reading Mass: Addison-Wesley Publishing Company, Inc. 1975

Maslow, Abraham. (1962). *Toward a Psychology of Being.* Princeton, New Jersey: D. Van Nostrand Company, Inc.

Masterson, James F. (1981). *The Narcissistic and Borderline Disorders, an integrated developmental approach.* New York: Brunner/Mazel

McGoey, Peter F. (2006). *Surrender: An Oasis on the Path to Recovery.* California Association of Marriage and Family Therapists 2006 Annual Conference. Audio Recording. Garden Grove: Mdrecordings@aol.com

Middelton-Moz, Jane. (1990). *Shame And Guilt, The Masters Of Disguise.* Deerfield Beach, Florida: Health Communications Inc.

Miller, Martin. (November 21, 2006). *Simpson book, TV plan dropped.* Los Angeles Times

Minuchin, Salvador. (1974). *Families and Family Therapy.* Cambridge, Mass: Harvard University Press.

Mitchell, Stephen. (2004). *Gilgagmesh, A New English Version.* New York: The Free Press.

Mushashi, Miyamoto. (1974). *A Book of Five Rings.* Woodstock, New York: The overlook Press

Nathanson, Donald, L. Ed. (1987). *The Many Faces of Shame.* New York: The Guilford Press

Ogden, Pat. (2006). Presented at a conference, *The Embodied Mind: Integration of the Body, Brain, and Mind in Clinical Practice.* UCLA, March 4 and 5

Osherson, Samuel, and Krugman, Steven. (1990) *Psychotherapy replicates a normal male struggle between connectedness and autonomy.* Psychotherapy, Volume 22/Number 3

Parachin, Victor. (1992). *Fears about tears? Why crying is good for you.* Vibrant Life, November/December 1992

Peck, M. Scott. (1987). *The Different Drum.* New York: Touchstone

Perls, Frederic. (1968). *Gestalt Therapy Verbatim.* Gestalt Journal

Porges, S. W. (2006). Presented at a conference, *The Embodied Mind: Integration of the Body, Brain, and Mind in Clinical Practice.* UCLA, March 4 and 5

Prabhavananda, swami, and Isherwood, Christopher. (1944). *The Song of God: Bhagavad-Gita.* New York: The New American Library

Robins, Richard W. (2001). *A longitudinal study of personality change in young adulthood.* Journal of Personality, volume 69, issue 4.

Schnarch, David. (1997). *Passionate Marriage, Keeping Love and Intimacy Alive in Committed Relationships.* New York: Henry Holt and Company

Schore, Allan. (2006). Presented at a conference, *The Embodied Mind: Integration of the Body, Brain, and Mind in Clinical Practice.* UCLA, March 5

Schore, Allan. (2003). *Affect Regulation and the Repair of the Self.* New York: W.W. Norton and Company

Shulman, Polly. (2006). *Crack me Up! Breaking the humor code*: Psychology Today: August, 2006

Siegal, Daniel J. (1999). *The Developing Mind.* New York: The Guilford Press

Siegal, Daniel J. and Hartzell, Mary. (2003). *Parenting from the Inside Out.* New York: Penguin

Siegal, Daniel J. (2005). *The Mindsight Lectures: cultivating insight and empathy in our internal and interpersonal lives.* Mind Your Brain, Inc.

Suarez, Edward C., Lewis, James G., Kuhn, Cynthia. (2003). *Hostility associated with immune function.* Monitor on Psychology, volume 34, number 3, March 2003

Taylor, Shelley E. (2002). *The Tending Instinct: How Nurturing is Essential to Who We Are and How We Live.* New York: Henry Holt and Co.

Tolkien, J. R. R. (1954). *The Lord of the Rings.* Boston: Houghton Mifflin Company

Tolle, Eckhart. (1999). *The Power of Now.* Novato, Ca: New World

Tourneau, Melanie. (2001). *Pump Up to Cheer Up.* Psychology Today: May

van der Kolk, Bessel. (2005). Presented at a conference, *The Anatomy of Intimacy.* Foundation for the Contemporary Family. UC Irvine, Nov. 5 and 6.

Wahoo, Jade. (2005). Personal communication, at a men's retreat on the green river

Watson, Jane Werner. (1956). *The Iliad and the Odyssey: the heroic story of the Trojan War and the fabulous adventures of Odysseus.* Golden Press

Wilber, Ken. (2000). Sex, Ecology, Spirituality, the spirit of evolution. (revised from 1995). Boston: Shambhala Publications

————. (2000). *Integral Psychology.* Boston and London: Shambala

————. (2000). *A Brief History of Everything.* Boston: Shambala

————. (2003). *Kosmic Consciousness.* Boulder: Sounds True (audio recording)

————. (2006). *Integral Spirituality.* Boston: Shambala

————. (2004). *The Simple Feeling of Being.* Boston: Shambala

Wiseman, Richard. (2003). *The Luck Factor: Changing Your Luck, Changing Your Life: The Four Essential Principles.* Miramax

Witt, Keith. (2007). *The Attuned Family, How to be a Great Parent to Your Kids and a Great Lover to Your Spouse.* iUniverse

Witt, Keith. (2006). *Sessions, All Therapy is About Relationships.*
keithwitt@cox.net

Witt, Keith. (2005). *Waking Up; Integrally Informed Individual and Conjoint Psychotherapy.* keithwitt@cox.net

www.aic.gov.au/publications/rrp/35/intro.pdf (2006). Disinhibition and Social Learning Models.

978-0-595-44731-2
0-595-44731-7